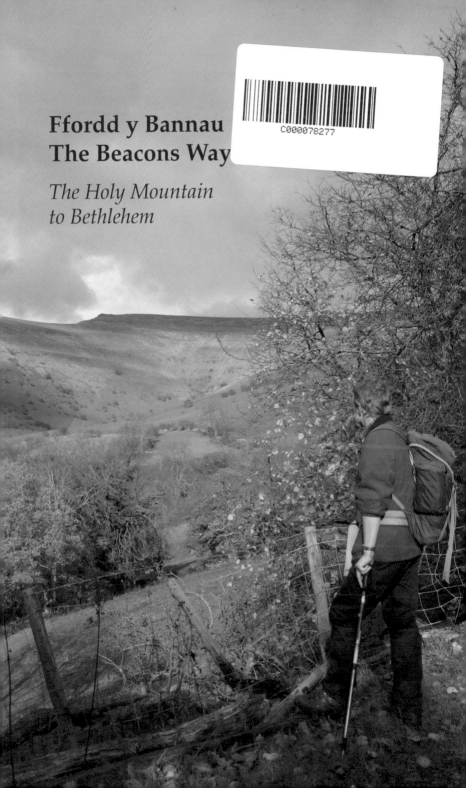

Ffordd y Bannau
The Beacons Way

The Holy Mountain to Bethlehem

Llyn y Fan Fawr

Ffordd y Bannau
The Beacons Way

The Holy Mountain to Bethlehem

*The Official Trail of The Brecon Beacons
National Park Authority*

Text by:
John Sansom & Arwel Michael
Photographs:
Chris Barber

Produced for the Brecon Beacons Park Society by:
Walking Wales Magazine Ltd.
3, Glantwymyn Village Workshops,
Glantwymyn, Machynlleth,
Montgomeryshire SY20 8LY.
Tel: 01650 511314

Published with generous grant aid from the Wales Tourist Board
Adfywio Scheme.

First published May 2005
ISBN 1 902305 35 4
© John Sansom & Arwel Michael 2005
Photography © Chris Barber FRGS 2005 unless otherwise stated

Cover photograph: The 'Diving Board' on Fan y Big
Title page: Looking into Cwm Mawr from the side of Cwm-gu

*Map extracts reproduced from Ordnance Survey mapping on behalf of Her Majesty's Stationery
Office © Crown Copyright 2005. OS Licence No: 100043446*

Printed by MWL Print Group Ltd. Tel: 01495 750033

CONTENTS

Foreword 6

Introduction 8

The Brecon Beacons National Park 12

The naming of the parts 13

Map of The Beacons Way 14

The Geology and Scenery 16

The Route: An Overview 28

The Route Guide

DAY 1   *Abergavenny or The Holy Mountain to Llanthony* 32

DAY 2   *Llanthony to Crickhowell* 45

DAY 3   *Crickhowell to Bwlch or Llangynidr* 61

DAY 4   *Llangynidr to Pen y Fan and Craig Cerrig-gleisiad* 71

DAY 5   *Craig Cerrig-gleisiad to Craig-y-nôs* 86

DAY 6   *Craig-y-nôs to Llyn Fan Fawr and Llanddeusant* 96

DAY 7   *Llanddeusant to Carreg Cennen* 112

DAY 8   *Carreg Cennen to Garn Goch and Bethlehem*
         (then on to Llangadog) 126

Tourist Information 134

Public transport 136

Brecon Beacons National Park Authority Visitor Services 136

Accommodation 138

Some further reading 139

Guidebooks 141

Foreword

THE Brecon Beacons National Park is a jewel in the crown of the UK's protected landscapes. It boasts some of the most spectacular upland formations in southern Britain, yet still remains one of the country's best kept secrets.

The Beacons Way makes history as the first official trail to span the entire length of the Brecon Beacons National Park. Although rights of way have always existed in the west, the National Park Authority had not previously promoted these because of the area's sense of wilderness and its huge ecological importance. However, with the arrival of Open Access in Wales on 28th May 2005, and with this new trail guiding walkers along a route which will minimise any impact on the area's ecology, the time is now right to launch the Beacons Way.

This exciting trail offers walkers a taste of everything that the Brecon Beacons National Park has to offer, from the lush green valleys in the (mostly English speaking) east, through to a remote wilderness in the (largely Welsh speaking) west.

In between you'll experience a host of contrasting landscapes, ranging from windswept uplands to reservoirs, ancient woodlands and breathtaking waterfalls. And the richness of this diverse landscape is matched only by the warmth and hospitality of the people who live and work here. Not bad for a walk in the Park!

Christopher Gledhill
Chief Executive
Brecon Beacons National Park Authority

Rhagair

MAE Parc Cenedlaethol Bannau Brycheiniog yn em yng nghoron tirluniau gwarchodedig y Deyrnas Unedig. Mae yma rai o'r ffurfiadau o ucheldir mwyaf ysblennydd yn Ne Prydain, ond eto mae'n parhau i fod yn un o gyfrinachau gorau'r wlad.

Mae Llwybr y Bannau yn gwneud hanes fel y llwybr swyddogol cyntaf i groesi ar hyd Parc Cenedlaethol Bannau Brycheiniog yn ei gyfanrwydd. Er bod hawliau tramwy wedi bodoli bob amser yn y gorllewin, nid oedd Awdurdod y Parc Cenedlaethol wedi hyrwyddo'r rhain yn y gorffennol oherwydd gwylltineb yr ardal a'i phwysigrwydd ecolegol enfawr. Ond gyda dyfodiad Mynediad Agored yng Nghymru ar 28 Mai 2005, a chyda'r llwybr newydd hwn yn arwain cerddwyr ar hyd taith a fydd yn cadw unrhyw effaith ar ecoleg yr ardal i isafswm, mae'n adeg briodol i lansio Llwybr y Bannau.

Mae'r llwybr cyffrous hwn yn cynnig blas i gerddwyr ar bopeth sydd gan Barc Cenedlaethol Bannau Brycheiniog i'w gynnig, o lesni ffrwythlon y dyffrynnoedd yn y dwyrain (sy'n Saesneg eu hiaith yn bennaf), hyd at wylltineb anghysbell yn y gorllewin (lle siaredir Cymraeg yn bennaf).

Rhyngddynt fe brofwch lu o dirluniau cyferbyniol, yn amrywio o ucheldiroedd sy'n cael eu hysgubo gan y gwynt, i gronfeydd, coedlannau hynafol a rhaeadrau sy'n ddigon i gipio'ch anadl. Ac mae cyfoeth y tirlun amrywiol hwn yn cael ei gyfateb gan gynhesrwydd a chroeso'r bobl sy'n byw ac yn gweithio yma. Dim yn ddrwg am dro yn y Parc!

Christopher Gledhill
Prif Weithredwr
Awdurdod Parc Cenedlaethol Bannau Brycheiniog

Introduction

IT was during the dark days of the Foot and Mouth disease outbreak in 2001 that this trail took shape. Throughout that period, access to the pastures and uplands of the Brecon Beacons National Park was, for the most part, totally forbidden for over six months. The impact that this closure had on tourism was considerable, and the value of tourism to the rural economy became starkly apparent.

Whilst the Foot and Mouth restrictions were at their height, The Brecon Beacons National Park Authority set up three working parties to look at the future for the National Park when the countryside reopened. Since the impact of the disease on tourism had been so great, one of these working parties looked at what could be done to restore, not just the status quo, but to consider what further boosts were needed to revive tourism in the area. The truth was that even before the outbreak of Foot and Mouth disease visitor numbers had been in decline, for a variety of complex reasons.

The Brecon Beacons Park Society was represented on these working parties. It was whilst a member of the tourism working party was telling the Executive Committee of the Society about the proceedings of the Tourism Working Party that the idea of a Beacons Trail was born. Most National Parks have specially dedicated trails, waymarked and promoted by a guide book giving information, not only about the route, but also about, for example, the archaeology, history, geology and folklore of area. The Brecon Beacons National Park has no such route. The Offa's Dyke National Trail goes along part of its eastern perimeter: the Taff Trail from Cardiff to Brecon uses two routes across the central Beacons: the Usk Valley Walk starting near Newport follows the Vale of Usk into the National Park. The Cambrian Way, a north-south trans-Wales route, still awaiting official recognition, gives walkers the most comprehensive view of the Park, but inevitably, with such a large remit and such a lot of ground to cover, it does not specifically explore the special features of the Brecon Beacons National Park.

The popularity of these trails is well attested. Those with 'National' status receive special funding. Such trails are hard to set up, and it was clear that to go for the national status would extend the period of gestation, and probably be beyond the ability of the Park Society to promote.

The Brecon Beacons National Park Authority has done a very good job opening up the rights of way within its boundaries. Furthermore most of the upland areas of the National Park are common land over which there are rights to roam. The high level of access already enjoyed would make the task of creating a trans-park trail much easier.

In the event, the process of getting the trail together took longer than intended. It is very much the work of two individuals. They apologise now for any misinformation or unclear guidance they have given. They also hope that they have properly acknowledged all sources of information.

Throughout the enterprise, the National Park Authority has been very supportive, and upon them has fallen the task of providing the waymarking to aid walkers in their passage across the farmland paths. The routes on the open hills and across commons are not waymarked. Such intrusive signing has never been the Authority's policy.

Credit must also go to Chris Barber, who has drawn on his collection of photographs, built up over 40 years, to illustrate this guide. He too has offered the project great support in so many ways and we are deeply indebted to him.

Special thanks are due to Nigel Phillips and Rob Knowles who tested out the route. It was Rob who led 25 walkers on the pilot eight-day trek which resulted in significant route changes. The Trail goes through two National Nature reserves and the Countryside Council for Wales has encouraged our use of these two sites. We have consulted the National Trust which owns the Skirrid and a large amount of the Central Beacons which we cross during the walk. They too have supported the project.

Finally, we must express our deepest gratitude to The Wales Tourist Board whose generous Adfywio grant made this whole venture possible.

Rhagarweiniad

YN ystod dyddiau tywyll Clwy'r Traed a'r Genau yn 2001 y daeth y llwybr hwn i fod. Drwy gydol y cyfnod hwnnw, cafodd y rhan fwyaf o'r mynediad i borfeydd ac ucheldiroedd Parc Cenedlaethol Bannau Brycheiniog, ei wahardd yn llwyr am dros chwe mis. Roedd yr effaith a gafodd y cau ar dwristiaeth yn sylweddol, a daeth gwerth twristiaeth i'r economi gwledig yn amlwg iawn.

Tra roedd cyfyngiadau Clwy'r Traed a'r Genau yn eu hanterth, sefydlodd Awdurdod Parc Cenedlaethol Bannau Brycheiniog dri gweithgor i edrych ar ddyfodol y Parc Cenedlaethol pan fyddai'r cefn gwlad yn ailagor. Oherwydd bod effaith y clefyd ar dwristiaeth wedi bod mor fawr, edrychodd un o'r gweithgorau hyn ar yr hyn y gellid ei wneud i adfer, nid dim ond y statws quo, ond i ystyried pa ysgogiadau pellach oedd yn angenrheidiol i adfywio twristiaeth yn yr ardal. Y gwir oedd, hyd yn oed cyn lledaeniad Clwy'r Traed a'r Genau, fod niferoedd yr ymwelwyr wedi bod yn gostwng, am amrywiaeth o resymau cymhleth.

Cynrychiolwyd Cymdeithas Parc Bannau Brycheiniog ar y gweithgorau hyn. Tra roedd aelod o'r gweithgor twristiaeth yn dweud wrth Bwyllgor Gweithredol y Gymdeithas am weithgareddau'r gweithgor twristiaeth y ganwyd y syniad am Lwybr y Bannau. Mae gan y rhan fwyaf o Barciau Cenedlaethol lwybrau wedi eu dynodi yn benodol, wedi eu cyfeirbwyntio, a'u hyrwyddo gan lawlyfr sy'n rhoi gwybodaeth, nid yn unig am y llwybr, ond hefyd am, er enghraifft, archeoleg, hanes, daeareg a chwedloniaeth yr ardal. Nid oes gan Barc Cenedlaethol Bannau Brycheiniog lwybr o'r fath. Mae Llwybr Cenedlaethol Clawdd Offa yn mynd ar hyd rhan o'i berimedr dwyreiniol: mae Llwybr Taf o Gaerdydd i Aberhonddu yn defnyddio dau lwybr ar draws canol y Bannau: mae Llwybr Dyffryn Wysg sy'n dechrau ger Casnewydd yn dilyn Dyffryn Wysg i mewn i'r Parc Cenedlaethol. Mae'r Cambrian Way, llwybr sy'n croesi o'r gogledd i'r de ar hyd Cymru gyfan, sy'n dal i ddisgwyl am gael cydnabyddiaeth swyddogol, yn rhoi'r olygfa fwyaf cynhwysfawr i gerddwyr o'r Parc. Ond yn anochel, gyda chylch gorchwyl mor fawr, chymaint o dir i ymestyn drosto, nid yw'n rhoi sylw yn benodol i nodweddion arbennig Parc Cenedlaethol Bannau Brycheiniog.

Mae poblogrwydd y llwybrau hyn yn amlwg iawn. Mae'r rhai

hynny gyda statws cenedlaethol yn derbyn cyllid arbennig. Mae llwybrau o'r fath yn anodd eu sefydlu, ac roedd yn amlwg y byddai mynd am y statws cenedlaethol yn ymestyn y cyfnod sefydlu, ac mae'n debyg y byddai hynny y tu hwnt i allu Cymdeithas y Parc i'w hyrwyddo.

Mae Awdurdod Parc Cenedlaethol Bannau Brycheiniog wedi gwneud gwaith da yn agor yr hawliau tramwy o fewn ei ffiniau. Ymhellach mae'r rhan fwyaf o ucheldiroedd y Parc Cenedlaethol yn dir comin y ceir hawliau i grwydro drostynt. Byddai lefel uchel y mynediad sy'n cael ei fwynhau yn barod yn gwneud y dasg o greu llwybr ar draws y Parc yn llawer haws.

Ond fel y digwyddodd pethau, cymerodd y broses o ddod ,'r llwybr at ei gilydd yn hwy na'r disgwyl. Mae yn ei hanfod yn waith dau unigolyn. Maent yn ymddiheuro yn awr am unrhyw wybodaeth anghywir neu unrhyw ganllawiau aneglur a roddwyd. Gobeithiant hefyd eu bod wedi cydnabod pob ffynhonnell gwybodaeth yn briodol.

Trwy gydol y fenter, mae Awdurdod y Parc Cenedlaethol wedi bod yn gefnogol iawn, a nhw sydd wedi cael y dasg o ddarparu'r cyferbwyntiau i gynorthwyo cerddwyr i fynd dros y llwybrau ar draws ffermdir. Nid yw'r llwybrau ar y mynyddoedd agored nac ar draws tiroedd comin wedi eu cyfeirbwyntio. Nid yw arwyddion mor ymwthiol erioed wedi bod yn bolisi'r Awdurdod.

Rhaid diolch hefyd i Chris Barber, sydd wedi defnyddio ei gasgliad o ffotograffau, a ddatblygwyd dros ddeugain mlynedd, i ddarlunio'r canllaw hwn. Mae hefyd wedi rhoi cefnogaeth fawr i'r prosiect mewn cymaint o ffyrdd ac mae arnom ddyled fawr iddo.

Hoffem ddiolch yn fawr iawn hefyd i Nigel Phillips a Rob Knowles a brofodd y llwybr. Rob Knowles a arweiniodd 25 o gerddwyr ar y daith beilot wyth diwrnod, a arweiniodd at wneud newidiadau sylweddol i'r llwybr.

Mae'r Llwybr yn mynd drwy ddwy Warchodfa Natur Genedlaethol ac mae Cyngor Cefn Gwlad Cymru wedi ein hannog i ddefnyddio'r ddau safle hwn. Rydym wedi ymgynghori ,'r Ymddiriedolaeth Genedlaethol sy'n berchen ar Ysgyryd Fawr a llawer o Ganol y Bannau yr ydym yn ei groesi yn ystod y daith. Maen nhw hefyd wedi cefnogi'r prosiect.

Yn olaf, rhaid i ni fynegi ein diolch dyfnaf i Fwrdd Croeso Cymru y bu i'w grant Adfywio hael wneud y fenter hon i gyd yn bosibl.

The Brecon Beacons National Park

THE Brecon Beacons National Park was created in 1957. It is one of a family of National Parks throughout the U.K. and one of the three in Wales. It covers land in what was then known as Monmouthshire (59 square miles), Breconshire (344 square miles), Carmarthenshire, (87 square miles) and Glamorgan (29 square miles). Since its formation new 'Unitary Authorities' have been created and then extinguished and recreated under new names with different boundaries. At the current count, the National Park's boundaries extend into nine different authorities, and who knows what the future will bring.

The formation of the Brecon Beacons National Park brought together areas which had, and still have today, distinct identities. The Brecon Beacons National Park is very much an artificial construct.

Before the creation of the Lake District and the Peak District National Parks, to mention but two, residents of those areas would have recognised that they were living in the Lake District or the Peak District. This was not the case in the Brecon Beacons National Park. Here residents, and visitors, are more likely to think of the Park, not in its entirety but in terms of its constituent parts. Llanthony residents will see themselves as living in the Monmouthshire Black Mountains. In the west of the Park, the reference point is Mynydd Du, also known as the Black Mountain or the Carmarthen Fans.

Visitors to the Llanthony Valley are surprised and puzzled to find that it is in the 'Brecon Beacons' or the 'Brecons' as it is sometimes called. News items describe events as happening in the Brecon Beacons when they really mean that it has taken place within the territory over which the Brecon Beacons National Park Authority exercises certain powers.

The powers exercised by all the Welsh National Park Authorities are in the process of being reviewed. At present there are two primary statutory functions:

1. To conserve and enhance the natural beauty, wildlife and cultural heritage of the Park.

2. To promote the understanding and enjoyment of the special qualities of the National Park.

There is a third purpose which they should also attempt to achieve 'without incurring significant expenditure', which is to foster economic and social wellbeing within the Park.

'The Beacons Way' which has the full support of the National Park Authority is very much a manifestation of the second statutory function of promoting understanding and enjoyment of the special features of this beautiful landscape.

So let us look at what the Brecon Beacons National Park is all about.

The naming of the parts

Those of us who have known the area for a long time, still think of the easterly upland block of the National Park as the Monmouthshire Black Mountains, (although most of the area is in Breconshire and a small part of it in Herefordshire). The central part of the Park was always referred to as the Brecon Beacons and the westerly uplands were known as the Carmarthen Fans, (although the highest point was in Breconshire). It is now politically correct to refer to the Monmouthshire Black Mountains simply as the Black Mountains. The Carmarthen Fans are now known as the Black Mountain or Mynydd Du. Between the Brecon Beacons and the Black Mountain (Carmarthen Fans) another area is distinguished. This is Fforest Fawr (The Great Forest), an ancient royal hunting ground. In the middle ages, its 40,000 acres would have been more wooded than now. The present area defined as Fforest Fawr is less extensive than the royal forest of the middle ages.

The most natural of all features links these four areas: it is their geology. And as you make your way about the Park it is the geology, and Man's often puny impact on it, that most effects what you see and experience.

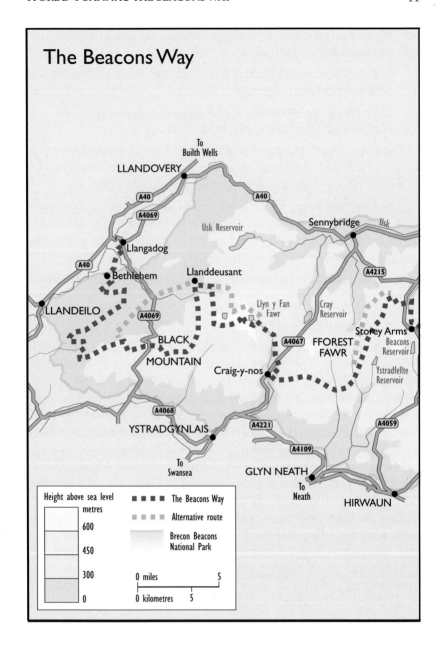

The Beacons Way

To Builth Wells

LLANDOVERY

A40

A40

A4069

Usk Reservoir

Sennybridge

Usk

Llangadog

A40

Bethlehem

Llanddeusant

A4215

LLANDEILO

A4069

Llyn y Fan Fawr

Cray Reservoir

Storey Arms

Beacons Reservoir

BLACK

A4067

FFOREST FAWR

MOUNTAIN

Craig-y-nos

Ystradfellte Reservoir

A4068

YSTRADGYNLAIS

A4221

A4059

To Swansea

A4109

GLYN NEATH

To Neath

HIRWAUN

Height above sea level
metres

600

450

300

0

■ ■ ■ ■ The Beacons Way

▨ ▨ ▨ ▨ Alternative route

Brecon Beacons National Park

0 miles   5

0 kilometres   5

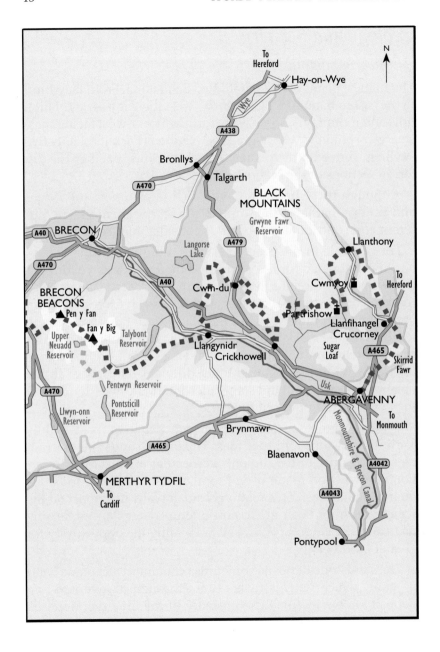

Geology and Scenery

Old Red Sandstone

The highest peaks are all of Old Red Sandstone. From Hay Bluff in the east to Bannau Sir Gaer in the west there is a series of high hills and mountains, some with north or north-west facing massive escarpments, which give the National Park its distinctive skylines. Indeed, it is this feature which pulls together the differing sections of the National Park.

Although these uplands have much in common, the ridges and valleys that lie to the south of the scarps are markedly different and contribute to the Park's considerable scenic variety.

For example in the Brecon Beacons a number of the valleys have been flooded for reservoirs and there is extensive forestry. In the Black Mountains, only one of the four large valleys has a reservoir and in that valley only is there extensive forestry. Farming is the predominant use of the Black Mountains valleys and foothills. In the Black Mountain (Carmarthen Fans) the country immediately south of the escarpment consists of Carboniferous deposits giving rise to an entirely different landscape. To the north is one reservoir and some forestry and farms extending to the northern boundary of the Park.

Old Red Sandstone deposits were quarried in the past, mainly for building stone and roof tiles. The use of sandstone for roof tiles is a feature of the region's vernacular architecture. Reservoir construction made use of local stone. Old Red Sandstone quarrying has been on a relatively small scale. Its impact on the scenery has not been great, and often provides an interesting feature in the landscape, as well as creating the opportunity for greater biodiversity.

The sandstone deposits sometimes contain a calcareous band of stone, which when streams drain through it, give rise to a deposit known as tufa. The presence of the lime rich deposits has an interesting effect on the flora, as has the alkaline waters of the springs. It causes acid-soil preferring plants to grow in close association with lime lovers. Sometimes these calcareous bands have been quarried, as at Henallt Common 1.5 miles 2.5

Brecon Beacons from Pen-y-crug

km south of Hay. The workings are visible on the southern boundary of the common and a ruined kiln exists at the western end of the deposit.

North-west of Capel-y-ffin, at the base of Tarren yr Esgob cliffs, there is a curious lump of rock, known locally as the Honeycomb Rock. It has fallen from the cliffs above, where more of it can be seen. The remains of a recently discovered small limekiln nearby shows that these deposits, like those at Henallt, were converted into agricultural lime for local use.

Carboniferous Limestone, Millstone Grit and the Lower Coal Measures

Along the southern fringe of the National Park, the Old Red Sandstone is overlain by Limestone deposits which vary in thickness and extent, and which are in turn, overlain by Millstone Grit.

The characteristic feature of this landscape is the pockmarked cratered moorland caused by the collapse of cave systems lying underneath the millstone grit. These sink holes (also known as swallow holes or shake holes) extend right across the Park's southern perimeter. In no other part of Britain are so many sinkholes to be found.

Cave systems abound. Over the millennia, streams have cut their way though the rocks, forming spectacular gorges such as the Clydach Gorge to the east of the Park and splendid water-falls on the rivers Nedd, Mellte and Hepste.

Limestone has been quarried over the centuries for building, industrial, civil engineering and agricultural purposes. The scars of the old and the new quarries are very much a feature of the southern fringe. Many limestone quarries have ceased opera-tion in recent years and some provide suitable sites for develop-ing climbing skills. The quarrying has sometimes provided cavers with new access to the cave systems.

Mynydd Llangattwg Limestone Escarpment

Sgwd Clungwyn on the River Mellte

The major caving sites are at:

- Pwll du – at the head of Cwm Llanwenarth 1.5 miles, 2.5km north of Blaenavon. This is the most recently discovered system and may prove to be the largest in the British Isles
- Llangattock Escarpment – Darren Cilau and Craig y Cilau
- Tawe Valley – Ogof Ffynnon Ddu and Dan yr Ogof Show caves

Cathedral Cave, Dan yr Ogof © Dan yr Ogof National Showcave

In the far west of the Park the carboniferous deposits were much exploited over the years to service the metal industries of the Swansea Valley in particular.

The Lower Coal Measures make an appearance, along the southern fringe of the Park, and despite much clearing up of slag heaps they are not a pretty site. Recently, open cast mining has impinged on the Park's southern boundary. An attempt to create a vast open cast mine just above the Clydach Gorge was fought off after a very long Public Inquiry. One area, just north of Blaenavon, has achieved the status of a World Heritage Site because of the importance of its industrial archaeology. Great things are planned for this area of industrial dereliction. In the west of the Park, between Ystradgynlais and Brynamman, local people are exerting pressure to restore their ravaged landscape and hold back further exploitation.

The Ice Age

During the Ice Age the mountains of the National Park generated glaciers and ice sheets which shaped the landscape within and outside the Park. The glaciers formed the cwms (or corries) that lie at the foot of some of the scarps. The little lakes of Llyn y Fan Fach and Llyn y Fan Fawr in the Black Mountain and Llyn Cwm Llwch below Corn Du and Pen y Fan in the Brecon Beacons are notable examples. There are many more such hollows.

Big Pit National Mining Museum, Blaenavon World Heritage Site

Llyn Cwm Llwch

Most do not feature lakes although they may well be very waterlogged and below the Langattock escarpment have given rise to a raised bog. Somewhat grander, is Llangorse Lake, formed by a gigantic glacial scoop.

Moraines, great piles of glacial debris, are a common feature of the landscape. One such moraine managed to divert the course of the River Honddu at the end of the Llanthony Valley as well as the River Monnow. It blocked their original course to the River Usk at Abergavenny, causing them to flow north, join up, and end as a tributary of the Wye.

The Post Glacial Period

Peat formation and degradation

The most important postglacial change to widely effect the landscape of the National Park has been the formation of peat deposits on the hills. These deposits have built up over the last 5000 years and support heather moors and grazing. Anyone familiar with the upland areas will know that in many places these peat deposits are eroding away and exposing the rock and thin mineral soils beneath. The causes of this erosion are many and varied, but man has certainly played a role in assisting it in some locations. Not only the heather moorland is under threat: the grasslands are also endangered.

Landslides

There are a number of examples of landslides, but the two most spectacular are those in the Black Mountains at Cwmyoy and on the Skirrid Mountain (Ysgyryd Fawr – The Holy Mountain). The one at Cwmyoy has an added interest. The ancient church (12th century) was built on unstable land associated with the landslide. Over the ensuing centuries, the church has bucked and writhed as the land has moved beneath it. Miraculously it

Cwmyoy Church in the Llanthony Valley

has not fallen down, yet! Its tower is said to lean more than the Tower of Pisa. Buttresses, stays and braces have been put in place to keep the tottering edifice from falling over.

Finally, the oldest rocks that appear in the Park must not be forgotten.

Silurian and Ordovician

Along, what can best be described as the Park's north-western boundary, the oldest rocks in Park make an appearance. The ridge of Trichrug, south-east of Bethlehem, is formed from rocks of the Silurian series which are typically shales and fossil bearing sandstones.

Although the National Park is more than its rocks, they, more than any thing else, shape the landscape and support, or challenge, man's presence in it.

The Prehistoric Landscape

FOLLOWING the retreat of the glaciers, the first identifiable settlers moved into the area covered by the National Park. Just south of the National Park, at Paviland Cave on Gower, evidence of occupation during the Ice Age was discovered, but no such sites have been found in the Park.

The Mesolithic 7500 BC–4500 BC

The first identifiable settlers left no monuments and the evidence that exists of their presence is mainly confined to worked flint tools. Waun Fignan Felin, the peat bog to the south-west of Fan Hir in the Black Mountain, has produced a quantity of flint, and analysis of the peat deposits has shown that clearing of the vegetation took place around this site, which at that time (about 7500 to 5500 BC) was a lake.

The Neolithic 4500 BC–2000 BC

The first structural remains we see in the Park belong to that part of the period which extended from 3500 to 2000BC. A number of these monuments are still very impressive. Perhaps the most notable is the chambered tomb at Penywyrlod (approx

1.4 miles, 2.2 km south of Talgarth). This was discovered in 1972 when the quarrying of a large mound revealed human skeletal remains, and a subsequent limited excavation confirmed seventeen burials. The tomb is 180 feet, 55 metres long, and 82 feet, 25 metres at its widest part. It would have stood 10 feet, 3 metres high. The tomb is in the care of CADW which is the Welsh equivalent of English Heritage. It can be approached by a footpath, but at the time of writing there is no on site interpretation.

A number of Chambered Tombs of this period are to be found in the Park but none lie on the route taken by the Beacons Way.

Standing stones, stone circles and stone alignments are associated with the latter end of the Neolithic and are also to be found associated with monuments of an Early Bronze Age dating.

The Bronze Age 2000 BC–800 BC

Whilst the Beacons Way does not go near any of the Chambered Tombs, it literally makes contact with many of the monuments of the Late Neolithic and Early Bronze Age.

This particular prehistoric period did much to shape the upland landscape we now enjoy. This period enjoyed a warm dry climate. Warmer in fact than we are experiencing today. Then the uplands were extensive areas of grassland and scrub providing good opportunities for hunting. Some areas, now open hill, were under cultivation. When the climate grew cooler and wetter the peat, which covers these uplands, began to form, perhaps, aided by over-cultivation and overstocking.

The use of the uplands for hunting is well proven in the Black Mountains where good examples of arrowheads and scrapers for dressing and cutting skins are frequently found. The Offa's Dyke footpath yields many such finds, washed out of the peat deposits to either side of the track during heavy rain. If you stumble across any, please note the location and donate it to Abergavenny Museum.

The most obvious monuments of the Bronze Age are the numerous round cairns, of all shapes and sizes that crown many of the summits and ridges of the mountains and moorlands of the

National Park. Whereas the chambered tombs were used for multiple burials, the round cairns of the Bronze Age were sometimes the graves of an individual who was probably a prominent member of their society. Other round cairns show signs of several burials taking place over a period of time. Most of these cairns were opened up by treasure hunters in times gone by and much material relating to them has been lost.

In addition a number of circular enclosures and field enclosure systems may date from this period.

It could be that the upland areas of the National Park were more extensively populated during this period than at any time before or since.

The Iron Age 800 BC–50 AD

The Iron Age is well represented in the National Park. Along the Usk Valley, on both its flanks, and on the high points above tributary streams such as the Clydach and Rhiangol, there are many hill forts and enclosures of Iron Age date.

Garn Goch is the largest Iron Age hill fort in Wales

On the first leg of the Beacons Way two such forts are evident. The first on the summit of the Holy Mountain – The Skirrid, which is a relatively obscure earthwork, and the second is the Pentwyn Hill Fort at the beginning of the walk along Hatterrall Hill. This fort is particularly large and its northern ramparts are clearly visible from the Hereford Abergavenny road.

On the second day the Beacons Way takes you to the impressive fort on the Table Mountain above Crickhowell. Here it is just about possible to pick out the circular foundations of huts that existed in the fort's interior.

On the final day of the trail, close by the hamlet of Bethlehem, you will walk through the largest hill fort in Wales at Garn Goch. Only a few paces from this fort (Y Gaer Fawr) lies a smaller fort (Y Gaer fach) believed to have been built at the same date. This is described in some detail in the text.

The hill forts usually consist of one or two defensive deep ditches of rectangular or circular shape. Some sites have more than one enclosure and were clearly enlarged after the initial construction. The wall on top of the ditch could be of stone and/ or a wooden stockade. The entrance was built in such a way as to deter invaders. These invaders would probably have been from neighbouring clans.

Most hill forts have no supply of water within them. They could not therefore withstand a siege. Many contain hut circles and were occupied all the time and may well have contained workshops of various sorts. Some of these hill forts are of a very grand design and one is led to conclude that they may have been early examples of conspicuous consumption aimed at impressing neighbours.

THE ROUTE: *An overview*

THE route of the Beacons Way is designed to present this beautiful part of Wales in the very best possible light. It is an area of high hills, deep valleys and expansive moorland. Traversing it will involve a lot of climbing, and the crossing of some very exposed upland. The route will not be waymarked over open hills and commons.

Good route-finding abilities are essential. Because the route goes into the hills, bad weather can have a very serious effect on the conditions. No person inexperienced in hill walking should attempt this trail unless accompanied by an experienced guide.

The trail sometimes goes off the beaten track, taking routes not usually explored by the average walker. The route is, for the most part, not too rough underfoot. It is neither an endurance test nor a mountain challenge event. It is within the competence of any fit rambler or walker accustomed to energetic hill walking. It is more demanding than walking in Exmoor, Dartmoor, the North York Moors, the Peak District and the Yorkshire Dales. It is not as challenging as Snowdonia, the Lake District or many parts of Scotland. When a section of the trail is particularly tough, the following day's trek will be less demanding.

The route is described in some detail, but the maps in the text will tell the walker more than words ever can.

Walkers will need the Brecon Beacons National Park 1:25,000 Ordnance Survey maps to enable them to see the trail in its full context. Without these maps, in bad weather or emergencies, it will be impossible to devise escape routes.

In the far west, on the final day of the walk, the current edition of the Central and Western National Park map omits a small section of the Park, and inevitably, the Beacons Way just finds its way off the map before swinging round onto it again. In this case, the map in the text will totally meet the needs of the walker.

The ability to read a map and use a compass is essential. The best of days can turn nasty, and even on a good day the summits may be swathed in mist.

DAY	ROUTE	DISTANCE MILES	DISTANCE KM	ASCENT FEET	ASCENT METRES
1	Abergavenny to Llanthony Holy Mountain to Llanthony	12.5 9.5	20 15	2680 2270	816 690
2	Llanthony to Crickhowell	13	20.9	2450	747
3	Crickhowell to Bwlch Crickhowell to Llangynidr	10.5 12	16.9 19.3	2100 2100	640 640
4	Llangynidr to Craig Cerrig-gleisiad	16.2	26.2	3788	1155
5	Craig Cerrig-gleisiad to Craig-y-nos	13	20.8	1970	600
6	Craig-y-nos to Llanddeusant high level Craig-y-nos to Llanddeusant escarpment base	10.5 10.4	16.9 16.7	2477 1591	755 485
7	Llanddeusant to Carreg Cennen	13.6	21.9	2570	783
8	Carreg Cennen to Llangadog	10	16	740	225

The most physically demanding section of the trail is on the fourth day: from Bwlch or Llangynidr to Storey Arms and Llwyn-y-celyn Youth Hostel. In adverse weather conditions, the alternative route, using part of the Taff Trail will make for easier walking but there is no way to miss out the ascent of Pen y Fan from the east.

The route from Craig Cerrig-gleisiad to Craig-y-nôs could prove tricky in thick fog. An easier route is suggested for that eventuality.

Llwyn-y-celyn Youth Hostel

Llanddeusant Youth Hostel

The routes from Craig-y-nôs (the high-level route and the alternative lower route that hugs the escarpment base) are easy to follow in fog.

The route from Llanddeusant Youth Hostel to Carreg Cennan castle is difficult in foggy conditions as far as the Brynamman road. An alternative country lane route is offered, which even experienced walkers might well prefer in bad weather. The route connects with the main route at a point where navigation presents no difficulties.

In designing the route there was a major constraint. The finishing point of each day's walk had to be at a location where accommodation is available nearby; or the availability of transport, public or private, to take the walker to nearby accommodation.

Two Youth Hostels feature on the route. Both close during the winter months and both are often fully booked. Advance booking is essential.

Note: From time to time footpaths are legally diverted and new permitted paths are created. When this happens on the Beacons Way Trail the resulting new route will be signed and waymarked.

**Ffordd y Bannau
The Beacons Way**

*The Holy Mountain to
Bethlehem*

DAY ONE

Abergavenny or The Holy Mountain to Llanthony

Distance:	*Abergavenny 12.5 miles/20 km*
	Skirrid car park 9.5 miles/15 km
Ascent:	*Abergavenny 2680 feet/816 metres*
	Skirrid 2270 feet/690 metres

THIS first leg of the Beacons Way takes you from the market town of Abergavenny into the Llanthony Valley in the Monmouthshire Black Mountains. There are two ascents, the first to the summit of the Holy Mountain and the second onto Hatterrall Hill.

The best option for the start of this trail is to get a lift or a taxi out to the Skirrid car park. There are no buses on this route. Otherwise, walk out from Abergavenny using lanes and a footpath across a golf course to reach the foot of The Skirrid Mountain (Ysgyryd Fawr) which has been known for many years as 'The Holy Mountain'.

Optional start from Abergavenny

The walk starts from the Tourist Information Office opposite the bus station. From there go up Cross Street and take the first turning on the right into Monk Street which proceeds to become Hereford Road. You will pass a fine church on your right. It is well worth a visit when you have a less urgent task to fulfil.

Continue along the road passing three sets of traffic lights and the fire station and turn right at Grosvenor Road, which is sign posted as leading to Skenfrith. At the end of Grosvenor Road, after it has dropped down and veered left where a road joins it from the right, take the first lane on your right. About 440 yards, 400 metres beyond where road and rail bridges cross over the lane, take the left fork. Continue onward passing a lane going to

your left, until some 550 yards, 500 metres beyond that lane you reach a sign posted footpath
on your left that crosses the Golf Course. Take
this path, and the necessary precautions to
avoid being struck by golf balls!

That path comes out on a lane. Cross the
lane and continue upwards, across the golf
course, to reach a footpath leading from
the boundary of the Golf Course. Continue along that footpath for some 650
yards, 600 metres in a north-easterly direction into the linear hamlet of Bryn-y-
gwenin.

Continue through the hamlet. Take
the first footpath to your left and follow it through to the main road. Turn
left at the main road, and after 440
yards, 400 metres you will arrive at the
Skirrid Car Park.

Recommended start from the Skirrid car park

The route from the car park to the

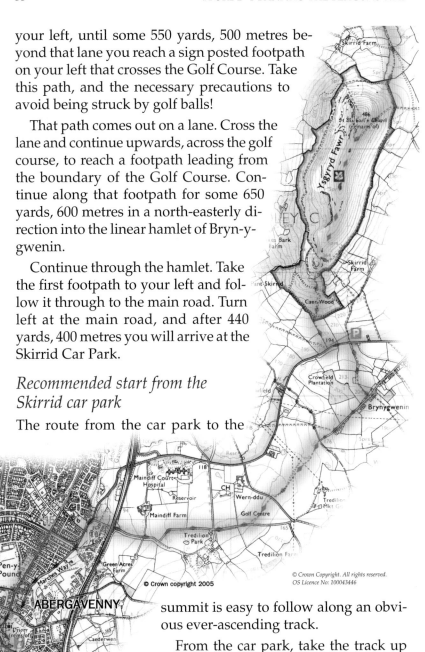

summit is easy to follow along an obvious ever-ascending track.

From the car park, take the track up
between the two planted hedgerows. Not

so long ago this was a much narrower track. The National Trust widened it and put in the hedging. At the head of this track, a gate leads into the wood. Take the path straight ahead of you that goes onwards and upwards until you come to another gate that leads onto the hill. Go through the gate and turn right following the well worn, and for part of its way stone pitched path, that heads up through scrubby woodland to the bare hill.

Press on for the next 1 km (0.6 miles) until you reach the summit.

> *William Coxe made his way to the summit in 1799 and this how he felt.....*
>
> *'....the effort I impatiently made to reach the summit (was) so violent that when I looked down from the narrow and desolate ridge, the boundless expanse around and beneath, which suddenly burst upon my sight, overcame me. I felt a mixed sensation of animation and lassitude. Horror and delight, such as I scarcely ever before experienced even in the Alps of Switzerland: my spirits almost failed, even curiosity was suspended, and I threw myself exhausted upon the ground. These sensations increased during my continuance to the summit. I several times attempted to walk along the ridge but my head became so giddy as I looked down the precipitous sides and particularly towards the great fissure, that I could not remain standing.' William Coxe 1799 From A historical Tour of Monmouthshire, Volume 1, 1801*

You, I am sure, are made of tougher fibre!

The Holy Mountain

Ysgyryd Fawr, the Big Skirrid, the Holy Mountain, are all names given to the lowest of the three great hills that stand sentinel over Abergavenny. It rises 1594 feet, 486 metres above the town, a long ridge, whose summit, at its northern extremity, harbours the ruined foundations of a small chapel dedicated to St Michael. The western flank of the ridge is scarred by a large landslide which perhaps occurred soon after the ice age glaciers retreated. This craggy landslide gives the mountain a cloven appearance. The welsh word 'ysgyryd', which is not in modern usage, almost certainly means 'split' or 'cloven.'

There are many myths and customs surrounding The Holy Mountain. One such myth declares that the landslide was caused by the earth-

Skirrid Fawr, also known as 'The Holy Mountain'

quake occurring at the moment of Christ's death on the cross. Another account claims that it happened when Noah's Ark passed over the hill. The red soil of the mountain was said to have been brought there by St Patrick either from Ireland or the Holy Land (there seems to be some doubt, but who can be certain after so many years). Farmers collected the red soil from around the mountain on Good Friday and scattered it on their land to ensure a good harvest. The soil was also placed in their coffins prior to burial. The chapel on the hill was in use until at least 1680. For centuries it was a place of pilgrimage. Pope Clement X in 1676 granted plenary indulgence to those visiting the chapel on the Feast of St Michael.

(For further information read 'The Seven Hills of Abergavenny' by Chris Barber)

In the vicinity of the chapel, whose remains are just visible, there is a monument to an even earlier occupation. It is one of the very many Iron Age Hill forts occupying the prominences of the hills in these parts.

The Skirrid Mountain, like its western neighbour The Sugar Loaf, is owned by The National Trust. In recent years the National Trust has acquired more land at both of these sites. On the Skirrid they bought the conifer plantation occupying its south-western lower slope. In time the conifers will be replaced by native broad-leaves and larch. Meanwhile new tracks have been cut through the plantation. In springtime, the flowers, particularly the wood anemones and bluebells, are outstanding. In early summer, the summit is carpeted with heath bedstraw, much dwarfed by its exposed position. This carpet can be so dense, that some years in suitable (calm) conditions, its normally imperceptible perfume fills the air.

When you reach the summit with its ruined chapel take time to enjoy the view. This enjoyment is not always possible. The ridge is very exposed and there are times when progress along it can be arduous against cross winds or head winds. It may not in fact be the windiest spot in Wales but it must be a strong contender.

The best way off the Skirrid is a little difficult to find. It is by an old track (marked as a footpath on the map) on its eastern side. The track leads off the summit ridge some 220 yards, 200 metres south of the ruined chapel, at a point where the surface has been pitted as a result of ancient quarrying.

The track leads down to the mountain fence. Look for a bridle gate, and take the footpath across fields heading in a broadly northerly direction. All the footpaths across fields are well marked. Your path takes you down through two fields with a small stream to your left. It then turns sharp left and leads to a stile by an old barn. Cross the stile, and then cross the field to the stile that leads onto the lane.

When you reach the lane turn right towards Pant y tyle and take the first signed footpath on your left. Having crossed the stile go down the field boundary until you see a stile on the right. Do not cross the stile but turn left and take the path that leads downward across fields into a small wood, over a bridge, out into the fields again and then by the side of a fence line to Llanvihangel Court.

When you leave the fields, a left turn takes you onto a rough lane skirting Llanvihangel Court, a fine late 16th century house with a very impressive barn which not so long ago underwent restoration assisted by CADW, the Welsh authority responsible for Ancient Monuments and much else besides. The drive to the house leads you to the main Hereford Abergavenny road. Cross the road and continue up the track into Llanvihangel Crucorney and should you feel so inclined to the Skirrid Mountain Inn.

The Skirrid Inn

There are probably a large number of inns claiming to be the oldest in Wales. But no matter whether the Skirrid can rightly claim this distinction its great antiquity is undisputed. It dates as far back as the 11th century. It was here that the beastly Judge Jeffreys held one of his bloody assizes. The chapel on the Skirrid was one of those places where the Catholics held their forbidden rites. One of their number was hanged from a beam above the stairwell of the inn. Time and numerous alterations have changed the exterior and the interior of this imposing building but it still has great character and comfort within. At the end of a winter walk, when the great hearth is ablaze with a welcome fire, it is as good a place as any to round off the day.

Skirrid Mountain Inn, Llanfihangel Crucorney

Working on the assumption that you visited the Skirrid Mountain Inn, turn left as you come out, then left again to take the road sign-posted to Llanthony. At the bottom of the hill take the right-hand fork and cross the bridge over the River Honddu. Take the first footpath on your left up to Great Llwygy Farm. It is well signed. (Take great care crossing the railway line.) On reaching the farm, turn left, and after a short distance, where the path divides, take the waymarked path on the right that rises steeply. On coming out of the wooded area onto open land, continue straight ahead. The line of the path drops down to a stile, and from that point the route is clear. This section can be somewhat rutted and muddy but you can walk to the side of the track with ease for most of its route. However, in the final section of the path, just before it reaches the metalled lane at Trawellwyd, it is often necessary to connect with the track (also a right of way) that runs parallel and just below it. It reaches the lane at a gate opposite Trawellwyd. It is on this high section that you get one of the finest views in the National Park. You can see north-westwards into the Llanthony Valley; and to the south-west, you have the view through Cwm Coed y Cerrig towards the mountains above Crickhowell.

On reaching the metalled lane turn left. When you get to the crossroads continue straight ahead, and after about 0.5 miles, 0.8 km go through the mountain gate onto Hatterrall Hill to join the Offa's Dyke National Trail.

The Brecon Beacons National Park Authority owns ten kilometres of this ridge, including land in Herefordshire. Having gone through the gate there are two things that deserve your attention.

The first is an information board put up by the National Park giving useful information about the hill. The second thing you might care to look out for lies just to the right of the gate and up the bank. It is the large northern rampart of the Pentwyn Iron Age Hillfort, known prosaically by the locals as the 'Fort Lump'.

Your route follows the Offa's Dyke path northward for 2.8 miles, 4.5 km across the heather moor.

The land you are on is common land, which means that there are

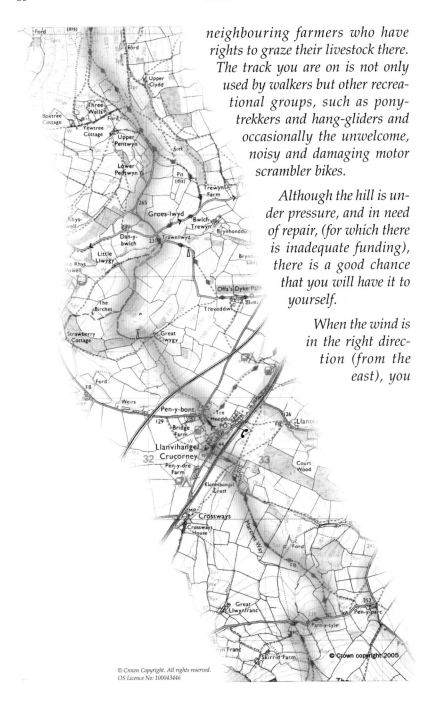

neighbouring farmers who have rights to graze their livestock there. The track you are on is not only used by walkers but other recreational groups, such as pony-trekkers and hang-gliders and occasionally the unwelcome, noisy and damaging motor scrambler bikes.

Although the hill is under pressure, and in need of repair, (for which there is inadequate funding), there is a good chance that you will have it to yourself.

When the wind is in the right direction (from the east), you *may find yourself surrounded by hang-gliders and para-gliders. Most walkers find their presence an added attraction but all do not share this view. Much discussion goes into trying to protect graziers' rights to avoid potential conflict between different user groups on a site like this. It is significant, that the main hang-gliding organisation, in order to guarantee the continued use of a take-off site, bought the Blorenge mountain, south of Abergavenny, when it came up for sale.*

The Offa's Dyke path along the ridge is waymarked by a series Old Red Sandstone milestone-like structures. The stone for these was provided by a small quarry below the Twyn y Gaer hillfort on the ridge west of the Hatterrall Hill.

The route takes you across a fine stretch of heather moor managed by the National Park for biodiversity. This involves the National Park Authority working with the Countryside Council for Wales, graziers, and shooting tenants to control the spread of bracken and encouraging a balance of young and old heather through a planned programme of burning and cutting.

This moor, like most heather moors, is a Site of Special Scientific Interest. Britain possesses some 80% of the world's heather moors but it is a habitat that is declining in area through the effects of excessive grazing, forestation, bracken invasion, natural, possibly climate induced degradation of the peat and in some areas of the National Park the uncontrolled illegal burning of the moors.

Walkers, riders of horses, mountain bikes, quads and scrambler bikes, all contribute to the damage. In this National Park, as in others, it is necessary, particularly where walking and recreational routes cross wet boggy peat-based heather moors, to construct firm tracks. This is done as much to protect the hills from the walkers as it is done to protect the walkers from the hill. Some people complain that these 'artificial' constructed paths detract from the natural beauty and wildness of the landscape. Others argue, that moorland and mountain tracks that grow yearly wider and deeper through man induced erosion, are equally intrusive, and that we owe it to future generations to reduce and control the unsightly impact that recreational use can have on the countryside.

So when you come to such constructed paths remember to make your impact on the hills more sustainable by using them.

The path from the Pentwyn hill fort ascends to a Triangulation pillar, drops slightly and rises again to cross the Cwmyoy spur. When it starts to descend, the Llanthony Valley is set out before you with the Priory visible in the distance. You proceed along the Offa's Dyke Path until just after it starts to rise again. At that point you will see a stone waymarker directing you down to Llanthony to the left, and Longtown,

to the right. Before you make the descent to Llanthony be sure to take the right turn and look down towards Longtown and the panorama set before you. To the west is Wales, where ridges seem to extend forever. To the eat, into England, is a purely pastoral landscape of farms and green fields ringed in the far distance by the 'blue remembered hills' of Houseman's poem.

It is a gradual and comfortable descent to the Priory. Where the route leaves the open hill there is a finger post directing you down. You go down a field, through Wirral Wood and emerge from the trees with Llanthony Priory just one field away.

Llanthony Priory in the Vale of Ewyas

Llanthony Priory

Llanthony Priory is a ruin of great beauty in a splendid setting. William de Lacey, a kinsman of a local Norman baron, came across the site round about 1103 when out hunting in the area. There was then, near the present Priory, a ruined hermit's cell, perhaps dating from 500 AD, said to be founded by St David himself. (Llanthony gets its name from a contraction of the Welsh Llan Ddewi Nant Honddu – Church of David on the river Honddu) The ruined chapel inspired William de Lacey to embark on a project which resulted in the foundation of an Augustinian Priory on this site.

The Priory was built in stages. In 1103 Ernisius, Chaplain to Queen Matilda, joined William de Lacey and they gathered around them a community of men who had chosen the monastic life. In 1108 a church dedicated to St John the Baptist was consecrated. By 1118 the community had become an Augustinian house funded by both Queen Matilda and King Henry I. Such is a brief account of how it all started.

The order suffered many vicissitudes. In 1135 a serious Welsh uprising began. The canons fled from Llanthony. First they went to Hereford, and then moved on to Gloucester where they established another priory which they named Llanthony Secunda. They did not return to Llanthony until about 1175, when with generous endowments from Irish estates, they began work erecting a church to replace the 1108 building. It was from 1175 to 1190 that work began on the buildings whose ruins we see today. Funds appear to have run out for a time but somewhere between 1200 and 1230 the building work was completed.

Six hundred years later in 1807 the Priory came into the news when Walter Savage Landor bought the Llanthony Estate that had come into existence at the time of the Reformation. Walter Savage Landor was a writer much respected by other writers in his day. He was a friend of Dickens and the Brownings. He lived from 1775 to 1864 but his time as master of Llanthony extended only from 1807 to 1813.

His time there was short but action packed. His efforts to set up a school at Llanthony were thwarted by the Church. The building of a fine house was made near impossible by jerry builders and the theft of materials. He employed lawyers who took fees and did little work. He was robbed by agents of the Prince of Wales of a fine flock of Merino sheep intended for Llanthony and could obtain no redress. He railed against local corruption without effect. This latter crusade was his undoing. Being unable to interest the proper authorities in the corrupt practices, he named a name. He wrote, and then distributed, a handbill through towns in the locality. The named man sued for libel and won the case and Landor had £800 damages to pay. His family took over the management of the estate and he fled to Italy to avoid paying the exorbitant damages.

The theft of the Merino sheep by the Prince Regent (later to become George IV) was not forgotten, and Landor's obituary for the Georges drove a nail into the coffin.

> *George the First was always reckoned*
> *Vile, but viler George the Second.*
> *And what mortal ever heard*
> *A good word of George the Third?*
> *When from earth the Fourth descended,*
> *God be praised the Georges ended!*

The estate remained in the Landor family until the second half of the 20th century. The last agent for the estate bought the Priory and the Abbey Hotel when it finally went up for sale. The ruin and the hotel remain in private ownership but CADW is responsible for the maintenance of the fabric of the Priory.

For further information concerning Walter Savage Landor see: *Landor: a Replevin. M. Elwin 1958.* The chapters that deal with Walter Savage Landor's brief involvement in the Estate are very entertaining whilst at the same time giving an unusually vivid picture of country life in the valley.

Llanthony Priory

DAY TWO

Llanthony to Crickhowell

Distance: *13 miles/20.9 km*
Ascent: *2450 feet/747 metres*

THIS part of the trail crosses three of the Black Mountains' four main ridges, and provides (if you are blessed by good weather) spectacular views of the Honddu, Grwyne Fawr, Grwyne Fechan and the Usk valleys. Additionally you will have the chance to see, although you do not visit them, most of the highest points in the Black Mountains. This walk is a great favourite of those who know the Black Mountains well.

The route starts at the hamlet of Llanthony at the junction of the approach road to the Priory and the road from Llanvihangel Crucorney to Capel-y-ffin. There is a metal finger post directing you to 'Bal Bach 2km' pointing you in the direction of a group of houses and outbuildings. One house, the 'The Mill', has a red post-box sunk into its gable end wall. The path you require goes in front of this house and leads to a metal bridge over the Honddu River. Cross the bridge, and then take the first stile on your right, and take the fenced off path up to the next stile. Cross the stile and the little stream and take the waymarked route up through the field. At the top of the field a stile leads into a wet area of rough woodland. You will come to a wooden sign-post, at which you take the path to Cwm Bwchel. After crossing a wooden bridge you leave the rough woodland behind you and enter a field with a waymarked footpath leading you up to the farm-house named Cwm-Bwchel.

To the right of the farmhouse, the path rises steeply to the top of the field where a stile leads into a conifer plantation. Con-tinue straight ahead. Another stile leads onto the hill, just be-yond which there is a finger post. You take the steeply climbing path up to Bal Bach. The stream is in a deepening valley to your left. Continue upwards for about 0.6 miles, 1 km, pausing often

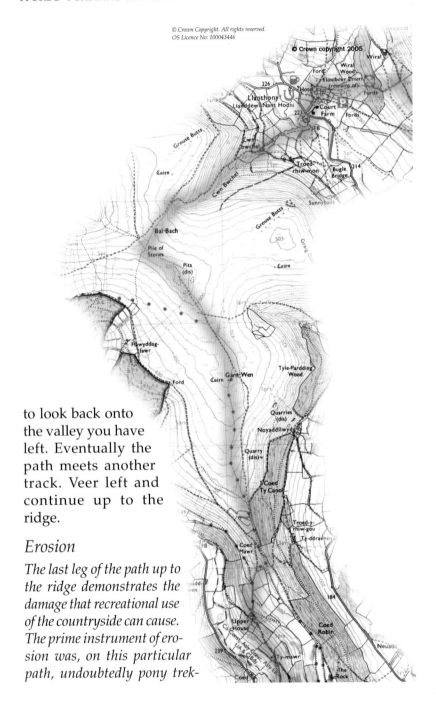

to look back onto the valley you have left. Eventually the path meets another track. Veer left and continue up to the ridge.

Erosion

The last leg of the path up to the ridge demonstrates the damage that recreational use of the countryside can cause. The prime instrument of erosion was, on this particular path, undoubtedly pony trek-

A bird's eye view of Llanthony Priory from Cwm-bwchel

king. The ponies' hoofs gouged into the peat surface creating a channel along which water draining off the hill could swiftly travel. Heavy rainfall caused this channel to become deeper and deeper. Walkers and ponies next walked on either side of the gully that was being formed. This widened the track further and caused even greater damage to the heather moor. It also created an unsightly scar.

The repair work on this track was carried out in the autumn of 2003. The work was largely funded by a substantial donation given to the Brecon Beacons Park Society by a firm of insurance brokers, The Marsh Group. The Marsh Group had staged outdoor events for its staff in the area and had become aware of the sort of damage that perfectly legitimate outdoor activities can cause. The money was passed to the Brecon Beacons National Park Authority, which commissioned the work which will put a halt to a problem that had worsened every year.

Once you reach the ridge, there is a panoramic view of the

Garn-wen

Black Mountains. The Skirrid to the south-east looks particularly good as does its near neighbour the Sugar Loaf. You are
also standing on very fine heather moor land which is being very
well managed and cared for by its owner.

On reaching the ridge you turn left and take the well-used
track that goes in a south-easterly direction. From hereon it is

downhill for the next 2.5 miles, 4 km, making the steep climb you have just made all the more worthwhile.

The main path leads to Garn-wen and a small tower-like dry stone structure of relatively modern date. It is built from the stones of the large Early Bronze Age cairn on which it rests.

From this cairn, the route proceeds downhill and reaches a point just south of an area marked as Coed Mawr on the map, and just after the forest plantation on your left. There is a small rough pile of stones in the centre of the main track supporting a stump of carved stone.

The Stone of Vengeance

This fragment of carved stone may be the remnant of a medieval wayside pilgrims' cross: alternatively, it may be, as is popularly believed, a monument commemorating the assassination of Richard de Clare in 1135. It is known locally as The Stone of Vengeance – Dial Cerrig. The story is that Richard de Clare was making his way from Abergavenny Castle to his property in Talgarth, when he and his party were attacked and slain by Morgan-ap-Owen, (the Welsh Lord of Caerleon) and his followers. It was an act of revenge for which the Welsh had very good cause; but that is another story.

You proceed from the Vengeance Stone by leaving the broad track that you have been using. Turn sharp right and follow the line of the wall down the western flank of the hill. Keep the wall on your left and you will reach a gate that leads onto a track between two walls. Go through the gate and follow the track down to Upper House farm and then the metalled road down to Ty Mawr Farm.

Ty Mawr

Ty Mawr is one of many very old houses that are to be found in the Black Mountains. The house we see today, together with its three-storey barn built into the steep bank, dates from the early 17th Century. Prior to that period an older house existed that was set at right angles to the northern end of the present building. It was built round about 1500 and the present building was put there as an extension to the original. Around 1600 there would have been a T shaped building on this site. All that remains of the early building is its substantial porch. This is incorporated into the newer building and now serves as a large walk-in pantry with some of its original features as a porch intact.

The older building became known when the present owner uncovered the foundations whilst carrying out essential drainage work.

It was only then that the full extent of the original building emerged. The walls of this ancient building are being consolidated to form a feature of one of the gardens.

Two substantial 13 feet, 4 metre high retaining dry stone walls have been rebuilt. The one at the back of the house was covered by earth, and was revealed during the excavations. It dates from 1500 and has been restored in its original style.

Continue down the lane beyond Ty Mawr, pass the Tabernacle Chapel and cross the bridge over the Grwyne Fawr River.

The lane rises steeply from the river to the main Grwyne Fawr road. Local people pronounce this word as griney as in tiny, and fower as in power.

For some 20 years at the beginning of the 20th Century, a light-gauge railway made its way from Llanvihangel Crucorney up to the reservoir workings at the top of

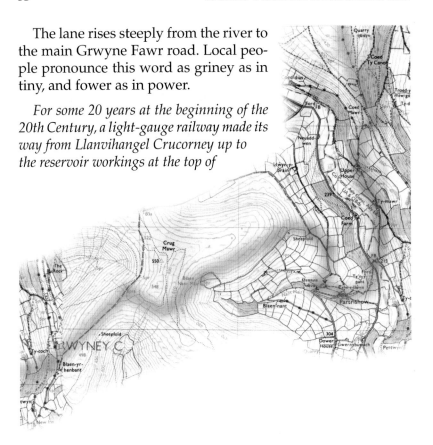

the valley. A temporary village was built there to house the workers and their families.

The reservoir inevitably flooded farmland. The extensive forestry plantations within the valley destroyed many other farms. Farming in this valley had long been in decline. The forester, who oversaw the planting of trees here, had farmed in the valley. It is to his credit that he took care to plant the trees around the farm houses in such a way that their ruins would remain a fitting testament to the generations who had lived and laboured here. Forty-seven ruined farms have been discovered and researched and their known histories pieced together. The work will in time be published and give us some idea of what went on in this now depopulated area.

Tyn-y-Llwyn Farmhouse

Almost opposite the point where the chapel lane meets the road you will see the stile which you must now cross. Follow the waymarked path that takes you up across the fields to yet another historic house. As you approach the house head for the gate just to the left of it. Your route takes you in front of the house.

Tyn-y-Llwyn

Whereas Ty Mawr has only recently been 'discovered' Tyn-y-Llwyn has the distinction of being named in Gothic script on the Ordnance Survey map. According to Richard Haslam, in the Powys volume of Buildings of Wales (Penguin 1979), it dates from the 15th and 16th century and was converted into its present cross shape in 1649. The house had remained in the same family for four hundred years until its recent sale. The house possesses many unaltered interior features. But to the walker approaching it from the fields below it is the splendid yew topiary which first strikes the eye. Next, it is the stone tiled roofs recently restored. And having taken in the fine house itself, the enormous flag-stones that form the terrace make you wonder what giants of men once worked here.

A few years back CADW provided funding for substantial restoration work to the house. But apart from the house there is a range of old buildings, including a cider press, in urgent need of restoration, for which funding has not been found.

Having passed the house turn right (rather than going straight on over the stile) and walk up by the garden wall and go through a gate that leads into a field. The well-defined field track rises up the field before dividing. Take the left-hand fork leading to the church.

Partrishow Church
'MENHIR ME FECIT I TEPORE GENILLIN'

This is the inscription around the rim of this church's simple stone font. Making allowances for the bad spelling of the 11th century stone-mason, it may be translated as:

MENHIR (the name of the mason) MADE ME AT THE TIME OF GENILLIN

Genillin was a Welsh prince who died c1065. This indicates that there was a church here around that date. All that remains of the original building would appear to be the north and south walls of the present nave.

According to tradition, this church commemorates a Celtic saint whose name might have been Ishow or Issue and whose history is unknown. It is believed that a shrine existed here prior to the building of the church. This would have been a site of pilgrimage, and the nearby Holy Well would have made the location doubly important. The western end of the church is walled off from the nave and the chancel, and is described as an Eglwys y bedd; literally 'church of the grave'. It is possible that the remains of the saint lie beneath the altar in this separate chapel that may have originally held the saint's shrine.

On entering the church through the 14th century porch, one is at first struck by its freshness and its light. Then one by one the special features emerge. First there is the simple but imposing font and behind it on the west wall the ochre painting of a Doom figure. The north wall carries a royal coat of arms, and together with the south wall, some beautifully executed texts from the Bible, the latter with corrections inserted.

Partrishow Church

The magnificent rood screen (circa 1500) is justly celebrated as are the Brute memorials that decorate the walls of the much restored Elizabethan chancel.

The Brutes were a family of farmers and monumental masons, who over several generations, lived and worked in the village of Llanbedr some 3 miles, 5 km south-west of the church. Their monuments are characterised by the use of brilliantly coloured dyes. The decorative motifs are flamboyant and baroque. The lettering is particularly elegant. Tulips are amongst the preferred floral decorations and cherubs abound. On the north wall of the chancel, the blue-robed angels are blowing golden trumpets with eyes bulging because of the effort. In other churches, the Victorian vicars found such monuments as these too cheerfully vulgar and had them removed from the walls. But here at Partrishow they have kept everything.

And when you leave the church going up the steps by the west wall, note the stone-tiled building with the mounting steps. Within that building there was a small fireplace so that the parson could dry his wet clothes during the service.

Although the church is remote it is still in regular use as the fresh floral decorations invariably attest. It is much visited by walkers, who time their arrival for the middle of the day, and sit on the stone south-facing bench (circa 1300) to enjoy their lunch.

On leaving the church turn right and go up the stone steps between the west wall of the church and the stone outbuilding, to the stile at the top of the bank. Cross the stile, turn right, and continue along the lane until you see a waymarked bridle way branching left off the road. Take the bridleway on the left and continue upwards. When you have passed through the gate onto the open hill you will see in front of you a small enclosed area used as a sheep fold. Continue ahead through the enclosed area and leave it by its exit against the dry stone wall to your right. For many years the exit point has been metal hurdles tied with binder twine. By the time you read this, a gate might be in place. When you leave the enclosure, turn left and follow the fence line up.

Turn left when you come to the top of the fence line, and take the track that runs parallel to the fence and wall. The track soon divides. Take the right hand fork. (Do not be tempted to walk immediately next to the wall). The track begins to rise and shortly divides again. Take the left fork that proceeds, at first, more or less parallel with the wall below.

At the time of writing, the Ordnance Survey map does not mark this track across the hill. It rises gradually and skirts the northern wall of the enclosure shown at Blaen Nant Mair. This enclosure would appear to be of great antiquity. What remains of it consists in part of large upright stones, rather than the more usual walls that are common to these parts. From this old enclosure, the track begins to veer to the right as it rises to go round the base of the southern end of Crug Mawr. The track meets up with a bridleway at grid reference SO258223.

At this point the view into the Grwyne Fechan valley is spectacular. Crug Hywel, (The Table Mountain), the next destination, lies to the south-west beneath Pen Cerrig-calch.

The sixteen mile, high level, circuit of this valley is one of the classic walks in the Brecon Beacons National Park. From this point, on a clear day, it is possible to make out practically every inch of the way.

On reaching the bridleway, turn left, and follow the track as it contours around Blaen-yr-henbant before descending to a gate above the old farm house known as Draen. At the gate, turn right, and follow the waymarked route down through Draen to the lane. (Do not go straight on to Henbant Fach)

At the time of going to press there is some discussion about exactly what line the path should follow. You will not go wrong if you take the waymarked route.

When you reach the road, turn right, and continue on the lane, until on your left, you will see a stile. Cross the stile into the field and take the waymarked route down, passing to the left of Llwynon. As the path descends, you will see to your left, the wooden bridge over the Grwyne Fechan. Head towards the bridge. This is a delightful spot and an ideal place to rest before the final stage of the day's walk.

Cross the bridge. The way up is well waymarked. After a steep ascent in a more or less northerly direction the path hairpins round and proceeds in a south-westerly direction before veering west through a field onto the road.

Table Mountain (Crug Hywel)

On reaching the road turn left. After about 220 yards, 200 metres, turn right at the house shown as Green Cottage on the map. The path goes up until, after a ruined barn and by a small conifer plantation, a gate leads onto the open hill. Go through the gate and turn right and walk a short way until you see a well-trodden track leading upwards to your left. This path will take you towards Table Mountain (Crug Hwyel). When the bracken is up, it is not so easy to take a direct route to the Table Mountain, but you will easily find your way there. On reaching the Table Mountain, climb the crag onto its summit.

There is an Iron Age hill fort on the summit of Crug Hwyel. You will have crossed the substantial ditch dug as part of its defences. It commands extensive views of the Usk Valley but having no supply of water it could not survive a siege. However, within the fort there would have been a number of dwellings and perhaps buildings serving other purposes. Such hill forts abound in the National Park and to either side of the Usk Valley they are particularly in evidence together with other, less grand, enclosures, which may be of this date.

If you are in need of another climb, you may feel inclined to walk to the top of Pen-Cerrig-calch (2300 feet, 701 metres), which lies immediately to your north. The track to the summit needs no description. It is best, should you attempt this, to descend the mountain by the same route.

The route to Crickhowell is, unsurprisingly, downhill all the way. The most beautiful way off is via Cwm Cwmbeth. Leave Table Mountain in a northerly direction and follow the mountain wall that curves round to the west. You follow this wall at first, but depart from its exact line on the well-used track, until, at the bottom of the cwm/valley, you will find a bridleway, to your left, coming onto the hill through sheepfolds. Go through

Crickhowel is famous for its 13-arched bridge

the sheepfolds and take the track between very substantial stone walls. For a short length, the route is on the same line as the stream. When it has been wet this can present a small problem. It is usually possible to keep your feet dry by moving to raised stones by the wall on your right before crossing the stream to a low bank on the left hand side. The path leads to an attractive upland pasture. Continue down this pasture, keeping a deeply sunken green lane (which eventually becomes a stream) to your left, until, after fording the stream, just before a bridle gate, the path enters into the woodland of Cwm Cwmbeth. Continue downwards, keeping the stream to your right until you eventually arrive at some stables and a modern barn. Just to the left of the stables you will see a gate and a stile. Cross the stile, veer to the left, and go through a gate that leads onto a housing estate. Continue straight downwards (an alleyway taking you between houses) until you arrive at the A40. Turn left for Crickhowell town centre, which is the end of this section of the walk.

Crickhowell

The official guide to the Brecon Beacons National Park published in 1967 by Her Majesty's Stationery Office begins thus:

> CRICKHOWELL. A small, sheltered, market town set between the lower slopes of Crucywel (Table Mountain) and the Usk......................The first local fortress was the Iron Age camp on Crucywel, and the first Norman castle may have been on the roadside mound a mile north-west of the town. The main medieval castle in Crickhowell controlled a large area, but now only its motte and bailey, parts of the curtain wall and a small round tower survive. Porth Mawr, on the west side of the town, is the great gate of a Tudor house of the Herbert family. The parish church of St Edmund, founded in the fourteenth century, contains much nineteenth century work. The pleasing thirteen arched and strongly buttressed bridge over the Usk was rebuilt in 1810. Gwernvale ½ m. northwest of Crickhowell, was the home of Sir George Everest...................'

Richard Haslam, (POWYS. The Buildings of Wales. Penguin/University of Wales Press) at the beginning of his perambulation of the town goes back to 1804, quoting a Richard Fenton who called Crickhowell ' the most cheerful looking town I ever saw'.

In a way that says it all; and 200 years later it is still true. The town looks very good indeed. There is a delightful jumble of buildings, prettily painted, many of which were built in the late eighteenth and early nineteenth century. And others, although possessing pleasing more modern exteriors, have interiors of greater antiquity. It also has shops still owned by local families and the familiar fascias of the average High Street are nowhere to be seen. You can eat and drink well here. There are hotels and guesthouses. You can provision here. You can do your Christmas shopping here. There is a small open market and a number of interesting shops to tempt you. Despite all this, it is not overrun by tourists, who so often pass through by the A40, on their way to somewhere else probably less appealing.

If by any chance you go down to the Usk Bridge try and work out why there are more arches on one side than the other!

The Bear Hotel in Crickhowell is an old coaching inn

DAY THREE

Crickhowell to Bwlch or Llangynidr

Distance to Bwlch:	*10.5 miles/16.9 km*
Ascent:	*2100 feet/640 metres*
Distance to Llangynidr :	*12.0 miles/19.3 km*
Ascent:	*as above*

THIS route explores the western flank of Pen Cerrig-calch and Pen Gloch-y-pibwr before crossing the Rhiangol valley at Cwmdu and making the gentle climb onto Mynydd Llangorse. It is a less arduous day than the two preceding sections of the trail. This route to Cwmdu has been chosen because it is so beautiful and presents an ever changing landscape which has the capacity to surprise. There is a tendency amongst hill walkers to stick to the ridges. Whilst high-level routes are very exciting, the views offered from mountain wall levels, often have exceptional qualities denied to those who prefer to keep their heads in or nearer to the clouds.

The walk commences from just before the White Hart public house on the A40 at the western extremity of Crickhowell (SO215191). Take the lane that goes up by the side of the White Hart.

There is an attractive shelter, recently restored, at the start of this lane. It has seats and a water fountain, (the latter not functioning) and is of late Victorian date. It was built as a place where citizens taking a constitutional, could pause and reflect, before returning home. Set next to the very hectic A40, it now is an unlikely spot to walk to, but the building graces this entrance to the town.

The metalled lane continues beyond Gwernvale Farm until, at a gate, it suddenly changes its character and is replaced by a track, ingeniously made of concrete sleepers, leading to Twyn. Just before you get to Twyn, cross the stile on your right into the field, and head up to a ruined barn. The path skirts the barn and some 80 feet, 25 metres beyond the doorway of the ruin turn left. You will see ahead of you a stile. Cross this stile and go up the bank to the right of the house. When you reach the top of the bank, turn sharp left, and after passing another ruined barn you will see ahead of you another stile. Cross this stile and proceed in a westerly direction, losing some height towards a group of imposing oak trees, and just beyond them you will pass on your right another ruined barn. The track you are on now joins the fence line on your left. The path drops down to cross a stream at a stile leading into a wood. Go through the wood, (the track is unmistakeable) and on emerging from the wood at a stile, continue in a westerly direction. You will meet up with a well-constructed track used to service the radio mast. Continue along this track, which runs immediately alongside the lower perimeter of a conifer plantation, before descending to a lane.

On reaching the lane turn right and take the first lane on the right (at Cwm Gu Cottage) which leads steeply to Cwm Mawr Farm.

View into Cwm Mawr

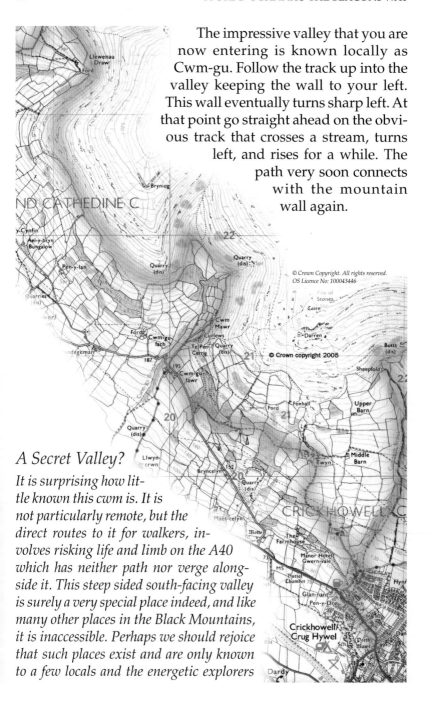

The impressive valley that you are now entering is known locally as Cwm-gu. Follow the track up into the valley keeping the wall to your left. This wall eventually turns sharp left. At that point go straight ahead on the obvious track that crosses a stream, turns left, and rises for a while. The path very soon connects with the mountain wall again.

A Secret Valley?

It is surprising how little known this cwm is. It is not particularly remote, but the direct routes to it for walkers, involves risking life and limb on the A40 which has neither path nor verge alongside it. This steep sided south-facing valley is surely a very special place indeed, and like many other places in the Black Mountains, it is inaccessible. Perhaps we should rejoice that such places exist and are only known to a few locals and the energetic explorers of the hills. At least this inaccessibility has resulted in the hawthorn bushes bearing an abundance of mistletoe which has not found its way to market.

In winter and spring sunshine, when the hawthorn is still bare of leaves, the bushes appear to be crowned with a golden halo of yellow mistletoe leaves.

Follow the wall to the next stream, cross the stream, turn left and take the track that leaves the boundary line of the wall, to climb in a just west-of-south direction, before meeting up with the wall again. The track then contours the hill following the boundary wall. At a point where a small stream crosses the path the boundary wall turns a corner and goes down hill.

Until recently the walker had to lose height here and follow the hill boundary line. In recent years the graziers have cut a broad swathe through the bracken and in so doing have provided an ideal route for walkers. So you simply carry on straight ahead through the line of the cut bracken, until in due course,

Cwmdu in the Rhiangoll Valley

the boundary wall/fence line track is re-encountered. The contouring continues for about a mile in a north-westerly direction. Then, it descends into a cwm, at the bottom of which is a farmhouse called Llanwenau Draw and the direction changes to north-east. Do not take the path off the hill at this point, but continue to follow the mountain wall up the other side of the cwm until you arrive at a stile (SO191238) which leads across a filed to Llanwenau. At Llanwenau turn left.

Just beyond Llanwenau, the path becomes a metalled lane. Turn right and continue down the lane. The lane passes by community woodland and swings round sharp left before meeting up with another lane. At this lane turn left and continue downwards into the village of Cwmdu where there is a pub and, at the time of going to press, a café.

Cwmdu Church

St. Michael's church, like Partrishow, dates back to the 11th century. However, when in 1831 the church was rebuilt, much of the older fabric dating from around 1430 was lost. In 1907 further rebuilding took place. Despite all this reconstruction some interesting features survive. Incorporated into the south buttress is a stone of great antiquity. It dates from the late 6th or early 7th century and is inscribed with the words CATACUS HIS JACIT/FILIUS TEGERNACUS (Here lies Catacus, son of Terganacus) as well as Ogam inscriptions. In the churchyard there is a Pillar Stone with a cross carved into it, believed to date from somewhere between the 7th and 9th centuries. The porch dates from the 15th century.

This church is especially remembered because in the 19th century the vicar in charge was Thomas Price, a bard, antiquary and scholar of the Welsh language and history. He pioneered the teaching of the Welsh language at a time when its study was forbidden in schools.

Directly opposite the pub, on the other side of the main road, there is a lane. Walk down this lane, and immediately after crossing the bridge, you will see on your right, a stile into a field. Two paths set off from this stile. You take the one that heads for the top left-hand corner of the field. Cross that stile, turn right and continue along the hedge line until a gate leads onto a lane.

On reaching the lane turn right and continue along it for about a mile up to Blaen-y-cwm-uchaf farm at the head of the valley. At that point a bridle-gate to your left leads onto the open hill. Go through the gate, turn right and take the track which climbs upward and connects with a north south bridle way across the hill. (It is worth remarking that there are more tracks on the hill than are shown on the map).

Bwlch, your next destination, lies at the southern end of this bridleway, and as you proceed along it, Llangorse Lake will come into view.

Llangorse Lake

Llangorse Lake was formed in the Ice Age by a giant glacial scoop. It is entirely natural and was, even in historic times, somewhat larger than it is now. The Official Guide to The National Park published in 1967 states 'This beautifully set lake is best seen from the surrounding hills', which is as true today as it was then. William Condrey, the naturalist writing in 1981, was very gloomy indeed about this lake. He was of the view then that it should be a National Nature Reserve to better protect its flora and fauna which was then being ravaged by all manner of polluting agents, as well as the water sports, including speed boats, which were likely to be damaging the habitats.

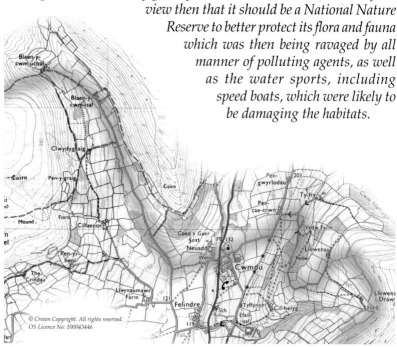

Llangorse Lake from Allt-yr-Esgair

It is one thing to a say that speed boats and noisy youths and kids enjoying themselves have a damaging affect on the wildlife and plants; but it is quite another thing to prove it. In fairness, the owner of the lake has done much to reduce the impact of 'unsustainable activities'. Furthermore, the National Park Authority has managed to acquire a large section of the southern shore of the lake. So things are moving in the right direction.

The circumstances surrounding the National Park Authority's ownership of part of the lake's southern shore are very interesting. In the late 1980s Ty Mawr farm, whose land went down to the shore, came onto the market. The farm had planning consent for a caravan and camp site. This consent had been 'used', but to not to the detriment of the quietness and appearance of this unspoilt side of the lake.

If a less scrupulous owner bought the farm, the chances were that the southern shore, with its reed beds and species rich meadows, could come under serious threat. The National Park and Powys County Council bought the farm, and then eventually resold it with a protective covenant on the way it could be farmed. The National Park Authority retained ownership of the shoreline together with some of the meadows. However, this meadowland was not fenced off, so that the existing field structure could be retained. Grazing of the land is carefully managed *to increase biodiversity. Since then the National Park has acquired further land around the lake which is managed as a reserve and there is no public access to it.*

The route you take hugs the fence and wall line until it drops down into a sort of funnel just above Bwlch. You come off the hill by a long white house set at a right angle to the track. Go down the rough metalled road that leads up to the house. When you reach the T junction turn right, and go a few paces, when you will see a foot-path going down between two stone walls. It leads to a chapel and its graveyard. Go through the graveyard and just below you is the A40 and the Morning Star Bunk House.

This could be a good spot to end this section of the trail. Accommodation is available in Bwlch. Buses run between Brecon and Abergavenny during the day except on Sunday.

If your intended destination is Llangynidr, cross the A40 (with great care), turn right, and just after the New Inn public house you will see on your left Darren Road. Go along Darren Road until its very end where you will see on your left a footpath going down by the side of the house. Indeed you may wonder whether this is the way you are meant to go! But it is. When you reach the road, two fields below, turn right, and go down the hill into Llangynidr.

You enter Llangynidr by crossing a superb ancient narrow stone bridge. Continue a little way up the hill and join the canal and head west as far as the locks.

Llangynidr

Llangynidr village is a mixture of the old and the new. But it is a village intensely aware of its past. In the year 2000, the Llangynidr Local History Society published 'Shadows in a Landscape. Llangynidr. The Evolution of a Community.' This is a 300 page, lavishly illustrated, account of the history of the village and the surrounding area. It is a model local history text.

In the summer of 2002 an excavation organised and financed by the villagers themselves uncovered the remains of a small Norman castle. The work on it will continue over further seasons. Another village project arising out of the Millennium was the restoration of the 5km of Dry Stone Walling that separated the common land from the farmed

Llangynidr Bridge spanning the River Usk

land on the mountainous terrain to the south of the village. That work is still in progress.

What the casual visitor is most aware of in the village is the river Usk with its splendid, but very narrow bridge, built between 1587 and 1630, and the canal. The Brecon and Abergavenny Canal came to the village in the late 1790s. At that time, as 'Shadows in a Landscape' records, the village had a population of 200 but as many as 600 workers were employed building the canal. We can only imagine what impact that must have had on the community. The purpose of the canal, which extended eventually from Pontypool to Brecon, was to bring coal and agricultural lime into the heart of rural Breconshire.

The hills to the south of Llangynidr are capped by carboniferous limestone, which further south again is capped by millstone grit. This limestone was extensively quarried along the southern rim of what is now the National Park. Sometimes limekilns were built on the quarry site and the lime produced would have been shifted down by mule cart. With the coming of the canal, tram roads, (horse drawn) were constructed to take limestone down to the canal side limekilns as well as take the stone to the valleys iron works where it was used as a flux. These same tram roads were used to transport coal down to the canal and in some cases iron products were brought to the canal for shipment to South Wales.

DAY FOUR

Llangynidr to Pen y Fan and Craig Cerrig-gleisiad

Distance: *16.2 miles/26.2 km*
Ascent: *3778 feet/1155 metres*
(The distance and ascent figures are for the
recommended route)

THERE are several options for this route.

The most arduous route over Tor y Foel and Cribyn adds 790 feet, 240 metres of steep ascent to the days' proceedings.

The 'Taff Trail', more gradual route, is 16 miles, 26.75 km long, and if the ascent of Tor y Foel and Cribyn are both omitted, involves 3000 feet, 911 metres of ascent.

This is perhaps the most demanding day of the whole walk. A prompt start is advised. This section of the trail takes us through the Eastern Beacons and into the Central Beacons. Rather inconveniently, it starts on Brecon Beacons Eastern Area map and moves onto the Central and Western Area map. The country becomes exposed, and in bad weather can be very wild and inhospitable, as can any high mountain and moorland. There are three significant climbs (excluding Tor y Foel and Cribyn). The first, from Llangynidr to Bwlch-y-waun just south of Tor y Foel is relatively gradual. The second from Torpantau, is very much steeper and more demanding. The third, up to the summit of Pen y Fan, is steep and coming at the end of the day, the most severe.

The start of the route begins at the canal at Lock 65 (just east of the road bridge over the canal) at the western end of the village.

Cross the canal by the wooden bridge at the lower lock gate and take the track immediately ahead that rises through woodland. A stile leads into a field and the waymarked path is straight ahead. To aim directly for the stile on the opposite side of the field head for the power line post in the centre of the field and the position of the stile in the hedgerow will be clearly visible.

After that, follow the waymarked route uphill across fields by Llwyn-yr-êos farm, then onto Pen-y-beili farm. On reaching the lane at Pen-y-bailey you have a choice of route.

Tough route

If you are feeling particularly fit and energetic, you might like to climb to the summit of Tor y Foel. The waymarked route up, initially a green lane, lies directly ahead. The views from the top are excellent but the climb is one of those dogged by false summits. The climb to the top is steep and about a mile and a quarter long, but it is rewarding.

If you take this route, when you reach the top, the only obvi-

ous way down (first south-westerly, then turning south) leads you to a surfaced road by a farm (Bwlch-y-waun) gate. Here it reconnects with the more gradual recommended route.

Recommended route

To proceed by the more gradual, less demanding route turn left on reaching the lane at Pen-y-bailey, and walk about 330 yards, 300 metres along the lane. Then turn right onto the signposted bridleway that rises steadily up to Bwlch-y-waun farm and continues beyond the farm as a metalled road. This road meets up

with the lane from Talybont at a gate
in a beautifully restored dry
stone wall. Go through
the gate and pause to
reflect on what lies
before you.

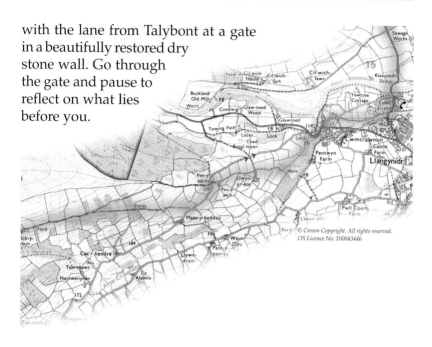

Dyffryn Crawnon Valley

Reservoirs and forests

Talybont reservoir lies below. It is one of sixteen reservoirs in the Brecon Beacons National Park. Most were built in the late 19th and early 20th centuries to support the increasing population and industrialisation of South Wales. This reservoir dates from 1927 and it supplies water to Newport and towns and villages along its route. The reservoir has become, along with Llangorse Lake, an important habitat for wintering water birds. Amongst these are goosander, widgeon, tufted duck, pochard, golden eye, and mute swan. Bewick's and whooper swans are known winter visitors.

As you can see, a large area of forestry surrounds the lake. The combination of forests and reservoirs transformed the landscape of the Brecon Beacons National Park during 20th century. The planting of these coniferous forests has of course been controversial. And recent years have seen changes in the Forestry Commission's policies. Open access is very much the order of the day, and a large number of forest trails have been created. Throughout the National Park, walkers and less energetic visitors have benefited from the car parks, picnic sites and other facilities that the forest authorities have provided.

Talybont Reservoir from Bwlch-y-Waun

Having gone through the gate to Bwlch-y-waun farm you turn left, and walk along the road for about 1 mile, 1.6 km until you reach the point shown on the map as Pen Rhiw-calch. Here you will find a memorial bench (on which to rest and enjoy the view) and a fingerpost pointing down through the forest to Abercwnavon.

The Bryn Oer (or Ore) Tram Road

Benjamin Hall, (of Big Ben fame) built, in 1815, a tram road, eight miles long, to connect the canal at Talybont with the Rhymney Iron-works. The lane on which you have been walking goes over the line of this old tram road. If you look, before going down to Abercwnavon, you can see where the track went under the road. The tram road is in the process of being restored and repaired so that walkers, cyclists and horse riders can follow its route up from Talybont to Trefil.

The fingerpost to Abercwnavon points your way down through the forest. About halfway down, the path crosses the eastern route of the Taff Trail, which, for the benefit of cyclists and walkers, links Cardiff to Brecon.

The Bryn Oer Tramroad

Turn left upon reaching the Taff Trail and take this gradually ascending route through the forest. After 2.5 miles, 4 km it emerges from the forest and connects with the narrow mountain road that links Talybont-on-Usk with Merthyr Tydfil.

An easier route

This is the better route should the summits be in cloud or the weather be generally bad.

On reaching the road, turn left, walk along the road for 800 metres, then turn right and take the Taff Trail into the forest.

Take the route through the forest for about 1 mile, 1.6 km, to the point where it joins the metalled road that leads to the Neuadd Reservoir. Do not take the reservoir road but take the well-defined waymarked track (actually classified as a Road used as

Public Path) that leads north to the gap (Bwlch ar y Fan) between Cribyn and Fan y Big. Locally this track is known as the Gap Road. It is closed to motorised traffic for most of the year.

At Bwlch ar y Fan the route connects with the main Beacons Way.

Recommended route

If the weather is good and you are feeling fit you should now begin your climb to the spectacular Beacons escarpment by scaling Craig y Fan Ddu. It is a steep ascent.

On reaching the road turn right and after a short while you will see a track, on your left, leading to a car park. Head for the car park and immediately you have crossed a culverted stream with an attractive waterfall you will see, on your left, just before the entrance to the car par, the route up.

Blaen-y-glyn waterfall

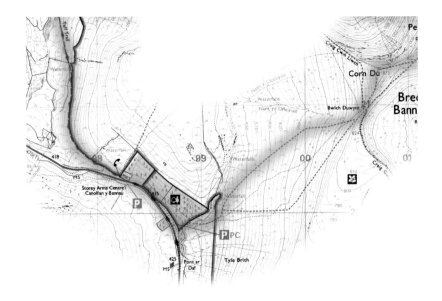

The ascent of Craig y Fan Ddu is one of the most popular climbs in the Eastern Beacons. For this reason the track up became seriously eroded. The National Park Authority has carried out much repair and restoration work in this area and the work is still far from complete. This is particularly so on the summit path that goes along top of the eastern escarpment.

The path starts by following the forest fence to the right and a series of waterfalls on the left. The route up needs no description or guide. The constructed pitched stone path leaves no doubt of the way to go.

On the way up you are almost certain to pause and take in the view. To the south can be seen a particularly severe case of erosion. This is on the slope of Pant y Creigiau and has been caused by the totally illegal use of scrambler motorbikes and even four wheel drive vehicles. This is a problem throughout the United Kingdom and what you can see on Pant y Creigiau is typical of the scarring such misuse of the countryside gives rise to. The police have taken action but the abuse continues.

When you reach to the top of the steep ascent of Craig y Fan Ddu take the track that follows the eastern edge of the summit

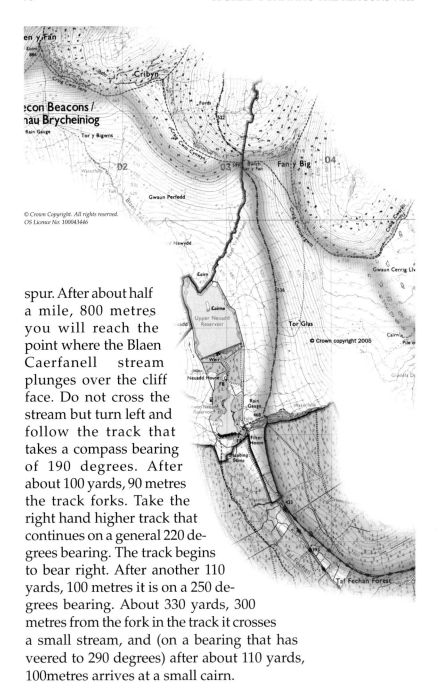

spur. After about half a mile, 800 metres you will reach the point where the Blaen Caerfanell stream plunges over the cliff face. Do not cross the stream but turn left and follow the track that takes a compass bearing of 190 degrees. After about 100 yards, 90 metres the track forks. Take the right hand higher track that continues on a general 220 degrees bearing. The track begins to bear right. After another 110 yards, 100 metres it is on a 250 degrees bearing. About 330 yards, 300 metres from the fork in the track it crosses a small stream, and (on a bearing that has veered to 290 degrees) after about 110 yards, 100metres arrives at a small cairn.

From this cairn the track takes a general compass bearing of 320 degrees across Gwaun Cerrig Llwydion avoiding all the peat hags and boggy ground to the right. Regular users have marked the route with small cairns along the first length of the route to Craig Cwmoergwm escarpment. Just before reaching the escarpment the track veers left to run parallel to it. At this point leave the track and stride out the 22 yards, 20 metres or so to the escarpment path.

Having reached the escarpment the route is plain sailing.

Your route to Pen y Fan is in a north-westerly direction along the cliff tops above Cwm Oergwm around to Fan y Big. Although you can omit the very top of Fan y Big it is worth walking the small extra distance to see the view from the out-jutting rock at its summit, known as the diving board,

From the summit of Fan y Big drop down to the pass on the 'Gap Road' below.

Taff Trail connecting point

In this part of the Central Beacons the National Park Authority has carried out extensive work on the paths to repair the scars that the thousands of stamping feet have inflicted on the hills. The main technique used is stone pitching, which involves driving stones into the hill to produce an effect similar to cobbling. Ideally, the stone should be local, to blend in with the terrain. If it has to be imported, it should be stone of the same type and appearance as the local stone wherever possible. More often than not, the stone has to be flown in by helicopter.

The National Trust owns the high land to the west of Fan y Big as far as the Merthyr Brecon road. Over the years, they have had a rolling programme of erosion repair work. This is carried out by well-supervised and trained volunteers who are based in the hostel style accommodation at Blaenglyn, the headquarters of the National Trust in this part of the Wales. If you feel like a working holiday why not get in touch with the National Trust at Blaenglyn. (telephone: 01874 622264)

There are two more serious climbs to go. If you decide to miss out Cribyn nobody will blame you. The toughest climb is to the summit of the highest peak in southern Britain: Pen y Fan (2906

The 'Diving Board' on Fan y Big

feet, 886 metres). And, whether you want to or not, there is no avoiding that ascent.

The choice is yours. You are meant to be enjoying yourself. Either stick to the escarpment all the way round or miss out Cribyn by taking the well-used track around its base. The climb to the summit of Pen y Fan is a strenuous affair but you can take your time!

Corn Du and Pen-y-Fan from Cribyn

Pen y Fan

Pen y Fan is the highest point in South Wales and South Britain. Because of its height and its proximity to a main road it is almost certainly the most climbed peak in the South Wales. Furthermore, the walk up from Pont ar Daf on the A470 is relatively gradual and people of a wide range of ability and experience are able to get to the summit. But here, as elsewhere, when the weather turns nasty it can be very challenging. In high winds in particular, the summit can be very difficult to approach.

Fifty years ago the way to the summit was not nearly so well defined. The summit was covered with grass and the now crumbling eastern approach to Pen y Fan was hardly eroded at all. It should also be mentioned that public transport access to the Beacons was much better than today. It was then possible to catch a train in Cardiff or Newport and travel to the railway station at Torpantau four miles south of Pen y Fan. It was possible to walk to the Beacons summits and then descend to Pont ar Daf for a nourishing meal at the café at Storey Arms. From there it was by bus back to Merthyr and down the valleys to Cardiff or Newport. Both the train and the café have gone!

Along the route of the Beacons Way you will have passed very many cairns dating from the Early Bronze Age. About four thousand years ago the climate of Britain was much warmer than today and many of the upland ridges would have been under cultivation or would have provided good grazing or hunting. The eminences of these hills and mountains were often chosen as burial sites for what might have been the more important members of the clans who resided here.

Pen y Fan, Corn Du and Fan y Big each had a cairn on their summits. Most of the prominent Bronze Age cairns were pillaged by treasure hunters many years ago. To add insult to injury that on Pen y Fan had a triangulation pillar erected on top of it. Because the visitor pressure upon the cairn was seriously damaging what remained of it, an excavation took place in 1991 to establish its structure and obtain dating material.

After the summit of Pen y Fan, the remaining Beacons summit, Corn Du, is but a gentle stroll across from the high point of the Beacons Way.

From the summit of the Beacons there are three ways down to the main road. After a good day out in the hills you will have earned yourself the privilege of taking the shortest route down. From Corn Du summit use the track that leads southward off its crag to Bwlch Duwynt. From there take the main track ('the motor way') down to the Pont ar Daf car park. You will be required to cross a shallow ford to get to it!

On reaching the car park (with toilets and burger van) turn right, and after leaving the car park walk northwards along the road to a large white building still called Storey Arms. It is not, you will sorry to learn, any longer a pub. It is now an Outdoor Education Centre.

Note: There is a regular bus service between Merthyr and Brecon that can be boarded at Storey Arms. There is also a more restricted service on Sundays.

Just beyond the Storey Arms, by the telephone box there is another section of the Taff Trail. Follow this route downwards. It is a very pleasant broad track, a little rough underfoot at first, but it soon becomes a green lane with spectacular views of the towering cliffs of Craig Cerrig-gleisiad.

View from Pen y Fan towards Cribyn

To the right of this track (actually the old road to Brecon) you will see a very long section of drystone walling. The National Trust began restoring this wall as part of a project that started around 1990. It used this wall in a government funded training scheme that aimed to revive the skills of dry stone walling in the area. The scheme's success is plainly visible in this length of old red sandstone walling. Today a number of trainees who were on this scheme are amongst the most sought after wallers in South Wales. Their skills, and their patrons' enthusiasm to see walls rebuilt, have resulted in the restoration of a number of prominent walls throughout the National Park.

A permitted footpath to the left off this major track will lead you to the Youth Hostel if that is your destination. Alternatively, a permitted path will take you across the valley directly to Craig Cerrig-gleisiad.

The route to the Youth Hostel is well signed, but there is a tendency for the small waymarking post to get knocked down by cattle. The important thing to remember is that having crossed the bridge you turn right and walk above the stream until you cross a small stream flowing into the main stream. You then head north-west to the top right hand corner of the field to the very popular and superbly situated hostel. Indeed whether you intend to stay there or not it is worth going to see it.

Craig Cerrig-gleisiad National Nature Reserve

DAY FIVE

Fforest Fawr:
Craig Cerrig-gleisiad to Craig-y-nôs

Distance: *13 miles/20.8 km*
Ascent: *1970 feet/600 metres*

NOTE: Unbridged stream crossing at the Blaen Llia car park. When there has been heavy rain, you are advised to take the easy/escape route given in the text to avoid the Blaen Llia ford.

Pen y Fan (and its associated peaks) is certainly the busiest and most often visited upland area in the National Park. By contrast, those hills to the west of the Brecon-Merthyr road, although equally accessible, receive little attention from visitors. This area is frequented by walkers anxious to get away from it all, who prefer to have a mountain to themselves rather than share it with all and sundry. You are likely to spend the whole day out and see very few people indeed.

And be warned! Although a large part of the route is on well-defined tracks there are some sections where this is not the case. The ability to read a map and use a compass is essential.

Craig Cerrig-gleisiad and Fan Frynach

Craig Cerrig-gleisiad is approached from a pull in/car park especially placed to give public access to this National Nature Reserve. It is one of six National Nature Reserves in the National Park, and you will traverse another such reserve before dropping down to Craig-y-nôs. Craig Cerrig-gleisiad possesses its 'National' status in part because it has growing on its north facing cliffs an arctic alpine plant, Purple Saxifrage, which is at the southernmost limit of its distribution in the British Isles. Peregrines nest here, Ring Ouzels are still visiting, and recently, another species more common in the north, the Golden Plover has been seen and its distinctive call heard. The area is of prime geomorphological interest. The behaviour of the ice during the last two glaciations has been much studied at this site and has been variously interpreted.

From the Llwyn-y-celyn Youth Hostel, a permitted path through deciduous woodland leads directly to the layby and picnic area for Craig Cerrig-gleisiad. Take special care crossing the busy A470 to get to the car park and the entrance into the Nature Reserve.

Enter Craig Cerrig-gleisiad and proceed upward on the main track to the dry stone wall with a squeeze stile. Squeeze through the stile and continue straight ahead.

(Ignore the signposted public footpath to the right which runs alongside a stretch of restored dry stone walling. The restoration was financed by the Countryside Council for Wales which owns and manages the site).

The route, through the National Nature Reserve, has permitted path status, and is provided by the Countryside Council for Wales as part of its open access policy in the reserves that you will visit as you walk the Beacons Way. The track is, for the first section, very well defined. When you reach the top of a knoll, (actually a glacial moraine) it becomes less clear, particularly when the bracken is up. The track leads to a stile, which you cross. The track then rises steeply following the right hand side of a fence. Follow it until the next stile, which is near a cairn. Cross the stile, and turn left following the waymarked track leading to another stile. Cross the stile, turn left, and head for the stile and gate, passing a pond on your right as you proceed.

Cross the stile and you are on the open hill. Turn right and follow the fence line (avoiding muddy bits), until you see, after a short time, a good track moving away from the fence line and gently rising. The track is on a general bearing of 230 degrees. Follow this track and where it peters out (across wetter ground) try to keep to this bearing.

You are in fact walking more or less parallel to the fence line above Cwm-du which, in a televised version of 'Lorna Doone', stood in for Exmoor. It was chosen because of its remoteness from road traffic and because few walkers venture hereabouts to interrupt the filming.

At this point you have to make a decision. The track that you are following is leading towards Cefn Perfedd that lies to the north of the Fan Dringarth and Fan Llia. If the weather is clear, these destinations are obvious, and the tracks to them are easy to see. If you cannot see your way forward the following route is recommended.

Easy escape route

If the weather is unfavourable, (or rivers are in spate) and you do not wish to test your navigational powers, you are advised to give Fan Dringarth and Fan Llia a miss and follow the fence line above Cwm-du which drops down steeply (passing sheep pens) to Sarn Helen. Once you have reached the rough track which is Sarn Helen, turn left and continue south-westwards. The rough track eventually meets up with a road.

Before you meet the road you will see on your right the massive standing stone known as Maen Llia. It is believed to be of Early Bronze age date.

Good weather route

Continue along this road until you reach a forest on your right. At that point you have reconnected with the Beacons Way.

If the weather is good the route to the summit of Fan Llia needs no description. The general bearing of 230 degrees leads

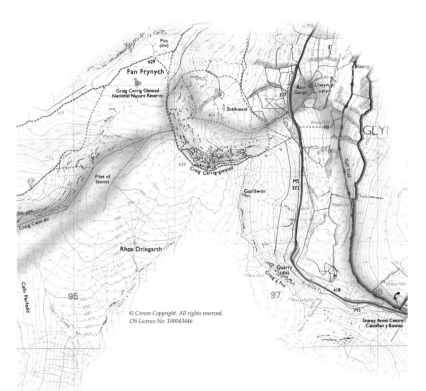

to Cefn Perfedd. You will, depending on the wet-
ness of the land, need to pick your way through or
round the streams that flow into the Nant y Gaseg.
When you reach the breast of Cefn Perfedd you will
see a faint track leading due south towards Fan
Dringarth. This track becomes clearer as you proceed
southwards and upwards. The summit of Fan Llia is almost 2 miles, 3.2 km away but the gradual ascent with
fine views all round makes this one of the most relaxing
climbs you could wish for.

When you eventually reach the summit (there is a rough cairn
marking it) you will see the track you must take leading down
in a south-westerly direction. Unfortunately this track does not
take you all the way down. You will need to find your own route,
skirting the heads of the streams that flow off the hill, until you
are nearing the fence line of the forest.

At the bottom of the hill there is a stiled path that takes you through the corner of the forest, to a ford, a car park and picnic site.

Ford the stream, climb up the steep car park access road, and join the Heol Senni (Senni Road) to Ystradfellte road at the top. Turn right and take the next turning on your left which is signed Sarn Helen.* This broad track offers a complete change of scenery as it rises gently through the conifer plantation.

Maen Madoc on the side of Sarn Helen

*Easy/escape route joins at this point

Maen Madoc

Shortly after you emerge from the forest you will see on your left, a Standing Stone, known as Maen Madoc. This is one of the few Standing Stones with a history in as far as it bears a Latin inscription:

DERVAC FILIVUS IVST (H)IC IACIT which means

(THE STONE) OF DERVACUS, SON OF JUSTUS. HE LIES HERE.

This is not exactly true since the stone was moved from its original position in 1940 from a position some 25 paces to the west of its present location. Prior to 1940 it stood directly beside Sarn Helen which is a Roman road. Sadly we do not know who Dervacus was or why he should have been accorded a 9 foot, 2.7 metres high monument. But spare him a thought as you pass by.

Having paid your respects to Dervacus continue along Sarn Helen. The road drops down to a river, the Nedd Fechan, which you can ford.

(Note: Should the river be in spate, there is an 'escape' route. Just before the ford, a track by Coed-y-Garreg farm leads down to the footbridge at Blaen-nedd-Isaf, where the Nedd Fechan can be crossed safely, enabling you to rejoin Sarn Helen at the fingerposted junction.)

Continue onward, until at the top of the rise you will reach a fingerposted junction.

Pant Mawr

At this point you take the footpath which leads in a north-westerly direction and is signposted to Penwyllt. Continue along the broad track until you see another signpost directing you to Penwyllt. The track now becomes a narrow moorland path. Very soon you will come to the substantial ruins of an old farmhouse and its outbuildings. This house, named Pant Mawr, was occupied until the early 1940s when it was demolished by friendly fire! The area was used as a firing range during the Second World War.

You are now traversing a fine heather moorland known as Pant Mawr. You have left behind the old red sandstone upland and you are crossing a plateau of limestone and millstone grit pitted by many shake holes.

The land is owned by the Cnewr Estate and has been the only upland area in the Brecon Beacons National where there has not been free access to roam and enjoy the hills. The path you are on is the only legal definitive footpath crossing the estate. However the nature of access to this land is being altered by a combination of the Countryside and Rights of Way Act and the estate's participation in Tir Gorfal, the Welsh agri-environment scheme.

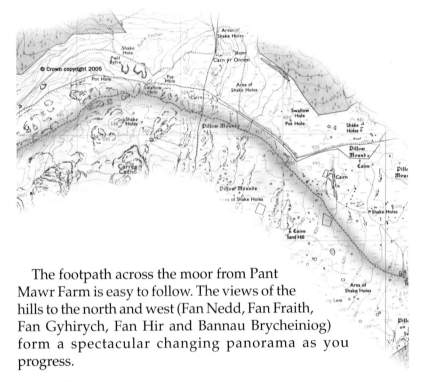

The footpath across the moor from Pant Mawr Farm is easy to follow. The views of the hills to the north and west (Fan Nedd, Fan Fraith, Fan Gyhirych, Fan Hir and Bannau Brycheiniog) form a spectacular changing panorama as you progress.

Rabbit farming

Between 1827 and 1860 this moor was used for the breeding of rabbits for their fur and for the table. The Ordnance Survey map shows a large number of features associated with this land use. A total of 694 hectares (1715 acres) were enclosed for rabbit rearing. At least 80 artificial warrens (pillow mounds) were constructed and within the greater enclosure a variety of other enclosures were built. The most intriguing of these are the small circular dry stone walled pits used as rabbit traps. These lay within small rectangular enclosures that may have been breed-

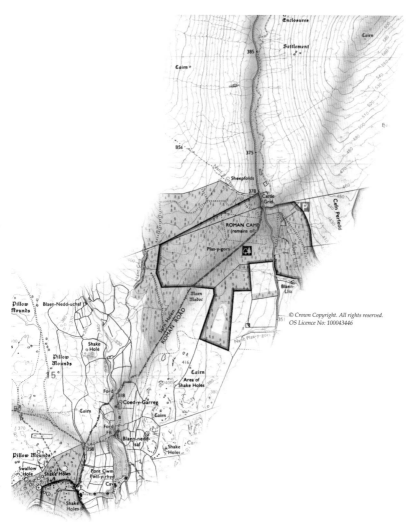

ing pens. There are five un-gated walled fields used for growing root crops as a supplementary feed.

This rabbit farm was one of three such farms on Fforest Fawr and is by far the largest. The other two, where there is no public access, are on Cefn Cul and south-west of Cray reservoir.

Towards the western end of the moor you enter an enclosed area which is part of the Ogof Ffynnon-ddu National Nature Reserve.

An example of limestone pavement, Ogof Ffynnon Ddu Nature Reserve
(BBNP Authority)

Caves and pavements

Ogof Ffynnon-ddu (Cave of the black spring) National Nature Reserve was designated to protect the surface geology, the limestone flora and the caves beneath. For many years the South Wales Caving Club has had its headquarters at the old quarry village of Penwyllt. They have extensively explored and mapped the caves of the area. The caves of this National Nature Reserve are managed by the Countryside Council for Wales (who own the site) in partnership with the South Wales Caving Club.

Within the larger enclosed area of the reserve is yet another enclosure that you are free to enter. This has been created to reduce the grazing pressure on the limestone pavement and to allow for the better development of the plant communities that exist there. Amongst the more interesting plants found are mountain everlasting, autumn gentian and mossy saxifrage. Thirty-nine species of birds and fourteen species of butterfly have been recorded here. The caves provide a home for rare invertebrates and moths.

As the path descends from the moor, the long terrace of quarrymen's cottages that now house the Caving Club, comes into view. Head for the right hand end of the terrace and you will connect up with a rough road that will take you to the road up to the quarry. When you reach the metalled road to the quarry turn left and go down it. Continue on the road until, having passed a bungalow on the right, you see a 'beware of falling rock' sign on the left and a bridle gate on the right. Go through the bridle gate and follow the path down to a road. On reaching the road, turn right, and when you reach the cul de sac, take the bridleway to the left of the house in front of you. Continue along the bridle way until the bridle way divides. You have a choice of two routes. You can take the bridleway to the left and head for the road over stepping stones or the bridge: or you can turn sharp left into Craig-y-nôs Country Park, owned and run by the Brecon Beacons National Park Authority, and make your way to the main road by that route.

Craig-y-nos Country Park (BBNP Authority)

DAY SIX

Mynydd Ddu:
Craig-y-nôs to Llyn y Fan Fawr and
Llanddeusant

High level route	Distance:	10.5 miles/16.9 km
	Ascent:	2477 feet/755 metres
Escarpment base route	Distance:	10.4 miles/16.7 km
	Ascent:	1591 feet/485 metres

THE first day of our excursion into Mynydd Du begins at Craig-y-nôs Castle, made famous by its legendary owner, Dame Adelina Patti, the great diva, who lived there from 1878 to 1919.

*The walk starts at the gates of Craig-y-nôs Country Park. Go through the car park and head for the Tawe Bridge by leaving the car park at its bottom left hand corner. As you cross the bridge, you will see on your left, Nant-Llynfell joining the Tawe immediately above the bridge.

The Llynfell issues out of the Dan-yr-Ogof cave system on the western flank of Glyntawe. Dan-yr-Ogof, (a Site of Special Scientific Interest) is the National Show Caves Centre of Wales. Past generations thought that the name of this stream should be Nant-y-Llyn-Pell (The Stream from the Far Lake) believing that its source was at Llyn y Fan Fawr. These days we know better.

Cross the bridge, turn left and continue upstream (with the Tawe on your left) until you reach the boundary of Craig-y-nôs Country Park.

To your left are large limestone stepping-stones for use when the stream is not in spate. Alternatively, a footbridge is provided immediately upstream, for the footpath that leads to the main road and the Dan-yr-Ogof Show Caves.

You might care to cross the bridge (a short detour) to see, on the far bank of the Nant Llynfell, an old flour mill.

*If the Country Park is closed continue northwards along the road to Tafarn-y-Garreg public house.

This mill is 'Melin-y-Blaenau' (The Blaenau Mill). It used to be called 'Melin-Caeth' (Lord's Mill). It was one of seven such mills in Wales. Farmers from a large area around were compelled to take their corn there for grinding.

The escarpment of Fan Hir

After this short detour recross the footbridge to the boundary of Craig-y-nôs Country Park.

The next stage of the route is in a north-easterly direction along the old Roman Auxiliary Road.

Eglwys Caradog

Immediately above you are the crags of Craig-y-Rhiwarth. Near its summit there is a cave named 'Eglwys Caradog' (Caradog's Church). Nobody knows how it came to have this name. There is an elaborate legend linking it with the Roman Emperor Claudius, Caradog's daughter Claudia, and St Paul's visit to South Wales with Claudia. St Paul's footprint is said to exist on Cribarth, the hill just west of Craig-y-nôs.

Alternatively, you might choose to believe that it should really be Eglwys Cadog, a fifth century Celtic saint noted for his learning. On the other hand, it could also refer to a monk named Caradog, who hid in the cave when he was in flight from his enemy Arglwydd Rhys of Deheubarth. The hills in this part of Wales are alive with legend.

Continue along the track that leads to Pwllcoediog farm, but do not go as far as the farm. Take the path on the left, with a kissing gate, and then follow waymarked path that passes a very large sink hole with a cave entrance and comes out by another kissing gate onto a road in the little hamlet of Callwen.

Having reached the hamlet of Callwen, take the path through the kissing gate on the right. Continue along the path through the field to Callwen church. The present church is not the original one and may not be on the original foundations.

The path goes through the churchyard. Near the entrance to the church there is a plaque commemorating the victims of an Anson aircraft that crashed on Fan Brycheiniog in December 1939.

Go through the churchyard on to the A4067 road and turn right. Continue along the road to the Tafarn-y-Garreg public house. This was a drovers' inn and was also used by limestone carters on their way to central Brecknock.

At Tafarn-y-Garreg, cross the road and take the track opposite which crosses the Tawe by a fine wooden bridge. Will Cefn-Cul, the old shepherd who used to live at the farm across the river, said that the bridge was built for his sheep and not for him.

You are about to leave Glyntawe and enter an area called Y Mynydd Du, The Black Mountain. It is an area where Welsh (Cymraeg) is the prominent language, and an area where the Normans had to fight hard to establish their ascendancy.

Having crossed the bridge, turn right and continue along the riverbank until reaching the gate at SN849173. Here, a green lane that leads you onto the mountain at a sheep pen. Having reached the open hill open, turn right and continue along the base of the hill in the direction of the escarpment (note: the walking can get a bit rough until you get to the end of the enclosed land to your right). When you come to the end of the enclosed land, and when you are well and truly out on the hill, you will see a track leading towards a stream called the Nant Tawe Fechan. Follow this track and when you reach the stream, at some waterfalls, (marked on the map) you will find a pleasant spot to take a break. It is usually possible to cross the stream at these falls. If that is possible, do so, and follow the stream up on its right bank. This is suggested because there is easier walking underfoot and the view of the stream is better from the right bank. If the stream is in spate, don't fret, but proceed up on its west bank.

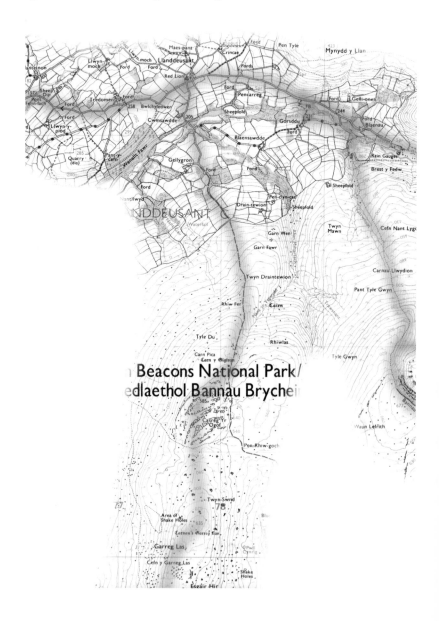

To your left, towering above, is the escarpment of Fan Hir (Long Peak). At the foot of Fan Hir there is a curious ridge, which has been variously interpreted, but is now believed to have been formed by a small glacier. This ridge, and you will walk along the top of it, is 0.75 mile, 1.2 km long. The full escarpment, and you will see it all, stretches for approx. 4.3 miles, 7 km as far as Llyn y Fan Fach.

Follow the stream upwards, and as it curves closer towards the foot of the escarpment, you will see the long morainic ridge. When you reach it, climb to its crest, and follow its switch-backing progress along the foot of the cliffs.

Geologists believe that at the southern end of the ridge there would have been a morainic dam, causing a substantial lake to form

between the cliffs of the escarpment and the morainic ridge. This was breached a long while ago but were it still to exist it would provide an interesting addition to the landscape.

Below Fan Hir

Continue along the base of the escarpment until, at that point, when you are wondering 'how much further is this lake?' it will come into view as you crest a small hill. Llyn y Fan Fawr – 'Lake of the Big Hill', is a moraine-dammed lake with a tendency to freeze over during the winter.

The water in the lake is crystal clear but unable to sustain fish. It is a home for leeches, which are often visible, so bathing is not recommended!

Llyn-y-Fan Fawr, with its broad and distant views, is an obvious place to take a break.

There are two recommended routes from here to Llanddeusant.

1. The high level escarpment summit route
2. The low level escarpment base route

1. The High Level Route
Fan Brycheiniog and Bannau Sir Gaer to Llanddeusant

This is very easy to follow but it involves two ascents. If there is cloud on top it is not recommended, unless you really wish to get to the summit of the Black Mountain.

At the south-west corner of the lake, a well-defined, much used path climbs to the escarpment. When you reach the top, at Bwlch y Giedd, you turn right and follow a path that leads you all the way round until it descends to Llyn y Fan Fach.

There is a short, but steep, climb out of Bwlch y Giedd to the summit of Fan Brycheiniog which at 2690 feet, 820 metres is the highest point in the west of the Brecon Beacons National Park. The views from Fan Brycheiniog are quite spectacular with Llyn y Fan Fawr nestling at the foot of the escarpment. Eastwards you can see Corn Du and Pen y Fan, and to the north-east, Y

Llyn y Fan Fawr (Lake of the Big Hill)

Mynyddoedd Duon (The Black Mountains). To the south and west you can see, across the Bristol Channel, to the west coast of England, from Somerset to Devon, and possibly north Cornwall and Lundy Island, on a very clear day.

Spend time taking in the view from Fan-Brycheiniog, then cross the summit plateau to Fan-Foel.

Flint flakes and a string of clay beads were found in the ruined cairn on the summit of Fan-Foel.

From Fan Foel, descend with care in poor visibility, down to Bwlch Blaen Twrch and Nentydd Blaen Twrch (SN816218) where the River Twrch has its source.

The meaning of 'Twrch' is Wild Boar, which will remind Welsh speakers of the story in the Mabinogion about Olwen and Culhwch and the Great Wild Boar hunt.

The Great Wild Boar Hunt

Culhwch wished to marry Olwen, but as is often the case in legend, her father was unwilling. However, her father was prepared to give consent providing the young man carried out a series of impossible tasks. The final task was to capture Twrch Trwyth a formidable wild boar. And so the chase was on! The young man pursued the wild boar with its seven piglets up hill and down dale through Pembrokeshire, Carmarthenshire, to the Vale of Loughor and the Amman valley and from there into the Black Mountain. By the time the hunt reached the River Twrch most of the piglets had been slain. Then the wild boar evaded capture by making its way down to the Bristol Channel and swimming across the sea to Cornwall. Here, with the aid of King Arthur and the Knights of the Round Table, the boar met its doom, and our hero got his girl.

The curious purpose of all this dashing about was to capture from the wild boar the razor, comb and shears that it kept between its ears so that Olwen's father could be certain of a good shave. Now that really does beggar belief!

There is a steep climb out of Bwlch Blaen Twrch to Picws Du and the summit of Bannau Sir Gaer (2457 feet, 749 metres). Below lies Llyn y Fan Fach.

View from Bannau Brycheiniog

Proceed along the top of the cliffs, passing the sandstone crags of Cwar-du-Mawr and Cwar-du-Bach. To the west, the Millstone Grit outcrop of Garreg Las, and the Limestone outcrop of Carreg yr Ogof, come into view across the valley of Twrch Fechan.

Having followed the track around the top of the escarpment and started to lose height, take the track that heads in a northerly direction across Carnau Llwydion.

It is shown on the map as a faint pecked line. The track leads to the right of a deep gully before making a steep descent across a spring line to a wooden gate.

In foggy weather, you are advised to take the very well defined track that descends to Llyn y Fan Fach and connects with the Water Board track that leads directly down to a tarmac lane, which then ascends to the Youth Hostel.

Go through the wooden gate and find your way down the

View of Llyn y Fan Fach from Bannau Sir Gaer

rough surface that is crossed and re-crossed by a stream. After a time the track swings left and the surface becomes rough pasture. This brings you to a gate onto a tarmac lane. Turn left along the tarmac lane, which leads to Gorsddu Farm. Just before the farm, on the right, there is a bridle gate into a marshy field. Go through the gate and find your way across the field, veering to the left to follow the line of an old mossy dry stone wall. You will cross a narrow stream, at least once, perhaps twice, depending which line you take over this meadowland. You will soon see the wooden bridge that you must cross.

Once across the bridge go straight ahead towards the fence. On reaching the fence turn left and take the track that rises following the fence line that is now on your right. This leads to a ruined barn. Take the track that turns right around the barn and having got to the end of the ruin you will see on your left a sunken lane rising steeply to a gate. Take this sunken lane. Go through the gate and climb up the steep bank to the road. On reaching the road turn left and continue along the steadily rising road which after about 0.75 mile, 1.2 km reaches the Youth Hostel.

2. The Low Level Escarpment Base Route
Llyn y Fan Fawr and Llyn y Fan Fach to Llanddeusant

There are two ways round the lake. Either take the track between the base of the escarpment and the lake, or follow the track round the eastern shore line. Both routes lead to Gwal y Cadno (The Fox's Lair) SN825223, where there is a ruined sheep pen with a shelter for the shepherd built in its corner.

From Gwal y Cadno continue along the base of the escarpment in the direction of Tro'r-Fan-Foel. Shortly, the Usk Reservoir will come into view in the north-east. Prior to reaching Tro'r Fan Foel, a depression called Gwely Ifan y Rhiw, can be seen

Bannau Sir Gaer

below on the right. This is a partial remnant of a 'U' shaped valley formed during the Ice Age. Translated it means 'The Bed of Ifan the Hill'. Perhaps Ifan was a shepherd who found this a desirable resting place during the Summer?

When you contoured Tro'r Fan Foel you crossed the county boundary between Breconshire and Carmarthenshire. Or should we say between Powys and Dyfed? Old habits die hard!

Continue along the base of the escarpment in a south-west direction. You can now see the majesty of Bannau Sir Gaer commanding the landscape of east Carmarthenshire, with the corrie lake of Llyn y Fan Fach nestling at the base of the encircling cliffs.

At Pant y Bwlch follow Afon Sychlwch down until reaching the feeder that contours the mountain gathering water for Llyn y Fan Fach. This feeder can be an invaluable friend during bad

Llyn y Fan Fach, famous for its legend of 'The Lady of the Lake'

weather, guiding walkers to Llyn y Fan Fach. The lake was used as a reservoir until quite recently, supplying water to Llanelli.

There is a strange puzzling legend about this lake.

Llyn y Fan Fach
The Legend of the Lady of the Lake

Towards the end of the twelfth century there lived at Blaensawdde, near Llanddeusant, a widow whose husband had died in the struggles of the princes of South Wales against the Normans. One day the widow's son, whilst tending his mother's cattle and other livestock at Llyn y Fan Fach, was astonished to see a beautiful girl sitting on the surface of the water combing her hair using the surface of the water as a mirror. Wishing to become better acquainted he offered her some of his bread and cheese. No doubt aware that there is no such thing as a free lunch, she declined his offer saying:

"Cras dy fara"	*"Your bread's hard baked"*
"Nid hawdd fy nala"	*"You don't catch me that easy"*

Then to his great disappointment, she sank back into the depths of the lake.

When he got home, he told his mother what had happened and she advised him to take some unbaked dough the next time.

Next day, before dawn, he went back to the lake hoping to see the girl again. He had to wait for a very long time until the girl re-appeared. He held out his hand proffering her some unbaked bread, and proclaimed his love. She refused both saying:

"Llaith dy fara"	*"Your bread's unbaked"*
"Ti ni fynna"	*"I will not have you"*

Then with a smile she returned to the depths.

He sat down by the lake and wept, much wounded by her rejection. When his mother heard the sad tale she suggested that next time he should take some half-baked bread.

Next morning he ran to the lake and waited for the reappearance of the girl. He waited all day and as night began to fall the most amazing thing happened. He saw cattle walking on the surface of the lake with the girl following behind them. She came towards him, and as she stepped upon the shore, she allowed the young man to take her hand. She took his bread and promised to be his wife on one condition. If, during their marriage, he were to strike her three times for no good reason, she would return to the lake forever. With that she disappeared into the lake.

Almost immediately two beautiful girls arose from the lake accompanied by a tall elderly white haired gentleman. The old gentleman spoke to the young man. He said that he could have the girl as his wife, providing he could recognise which of the two identical girls who stood before him, was the one he had fallen in love with. In truth, they were so much alike that the young man was in a state of despair. Then one of the girls moved her foot slightly forward. It was her that he chose, and he had chosen correctly.

The old man said that her dowry would be as many sheep, cattle, goats and horses as she could count in one breath. Then he reminded the young man, should he strike his wife on three separate occasions, for no good reason, she would return to the lake forever taking all the animals with her.

The Lady of the Lake counted as fast as she could, and the animals came out of the lake as fast as she counted. The couple lived happily for many years in the farm called Esgair-Llaethdy, a mile from Myddfai, which is there to this day and still inhabited.

And she bore her husband three sons.

It happened that they were invited to a christening in the district. She complained to her husband that the journey was too far to walk. He told her to get the horse from the field whilst he went into the house to fetch her gloves. On returning, he noticed that she had not collected the horse and he lightly tapped her on the shoulder with the gloves, saying 'Come, come!' She reminded him of his wedding vows, for he had now struck her for the first time.

Some time later, when they were guests at a wedding, she started crying. Her husband tapped her on her shoulder and asked why she was crying. She replied saying that she was sad because the trials and tribulations of the young couple would soon be starting. Then she re-

minded him that his troubles would soon be starting unless he was more careful. He had struck her for the second time!

Years passed and the sons grew to be healthy and wise. Then, whilst at a funeral, the wife suddenly started laughing. Her husband touched her on the shoulder and asked her to be quiet. 'When people die, then they are out of their misery' she said 'and you have struck the final blow!' She left the funeral and, returning home, called all the animals, by their names, to follow her. She bade her husband farewell and walked towards the lake calling in the animals all the time.

Four oxen ploughing the field, responded to her call. They followed her across the mountain, still drawing the plough, and cut such a deep furrow that it is to be seen to this day.

For years, her sons searched for their mother by the lakeside. Then one day, many years later, she appeared before the eldest son Rhiwallon and granted him the gift of healing the sick. He became physician to Rhys Gryg, Prince of Dinefwr and his sons followed after him. It is believed that their skills and knowledge formed the foundation for the work of the Physicians of Myddfai. But that is another story!

Leave the lake by the track leading in a northerly direction from the dam. The stream flowing out of the dam is the Afon Sawdde. The track passes the old filter beds on the left, currently used as a salmon and trout hatchery. Continuing down into the valley you pass on the right the old water works house called Blaenau. Continue along this track which ends at a cattle grid, and then continue along the tarmac road for 1.25 miles, 2 km until you reach Llanddeusant Church and Youth hostel.

DAY SEVEN

Mynydd Ddu:
Llanddeusant to Carreg Cennen

Distance: *13.6 miles/21.9 km*
Ascent: *2570 feet/783 metres*

THE second day of our journey across the Black Mountain takes us through one of the least walked parts of the National Park and requires good map reading ability for the section from Llanddeusant to Pen-Rhiw-Wen. To aid navigation grid references are frequently used in the text.

Bad weather and restricted visibility route: Llanddeusant to brest Cwm Llwyd & Carreg Cennen 11 miles (see map on pages 114–115)

All walkers are advised to consider using this route when adverse conditions call for a very high level of navigational skill. This alternative route uses attractive country lanes and eventually connects with the fair weather route.

From the Youth Hostel take the lane that goes in a general westerly direction to Twynllanan (SN754244). (Alternatively from the Cross Inn take the road heading south-west to Twynllanan.)

At Twynllanan take the lane that heads south-west to Nant-gwynne SN755241 and then to Hen-bont. From Hen-bont head for Pont Newydd on the main road A4069. Cross the road and take the minor road to Capel-Gwynfe. At Capel-Gwynfe continue in a south-westerly direction. You will come to cross roads after just over a kilometre. Go straight across and continue for about 1 mile, 1.6 km until the road forks.

Take the left fork which will lead you up to the mountain at Brest Cwm Llwyd where it connects with the fair weather route.

Llanddeusant Youth Hostel to the Brynamman Road

Distance: *approx 7.25 miles/11.5 km*
Ascent: *approx 2075 feet/633 metres*
(see map on pages 116–117)

Leave the Youth Hostel and head due south down the metalled lane to the Sawdde Bridge.

From this bridge, you begin the longest (1.9 miles, 3km) and the greatest ascent (1245 feet, 380 metres) of the day.

To Carreg Yr Ogof

Cross the bridge and continue up the road (ignoring the signed footpath on the left to Blaensawdde Farm). There is a sign on the

Crossing the limestone summit of Carreg yr Ogof

right hand side of the road that says Gellygron Farm. On crest-
ing the hill, and just before Gellygron Farm, you leave the
metalled road and take the bridleway that leads up to the mountain fence. This bridleway is rough under foot. Very stony and
in wet weather it is somewhat slippery underfoot. It is not very
comfortable to the walker.

*During the Industrial Revolution this ancient way saw many fu-
neral processions from Ystradgynlais to Llanddeusant. They were the
funerals of Llanddeusant men who had crossed the mountain to live
and work in the coalfields in and around Ystradgynlais. It was often
their wish to be buried back in Llanddeusant. A messenger would be
sent over the mountain to arrange the date and time of the funeral. The
coffined body was conveyed to Aberdeudwrch, in the heart of The
Black Mountain, (SN785186) where the people of Llanddeusant
were waiting to receive the body of one of their sons on its
final journey home.*

You will follow in their footsteps as far as Carreg
Yr Ogof.

Part way up the hill the worn track veers
to the right. Make certain you continue
straight on upwards. The line of the
bridleway is signed. Eventually you will reach a gate
and a stile that leads
onto the open hill.

Bad weather – restricted visibility route

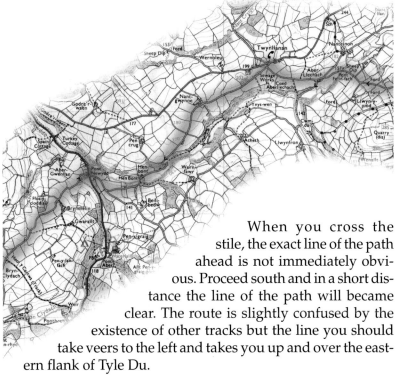

When you cross the stile, the exact line of the path ahead is not immediately obvious. Proceed south and in a short distance the line of the path will became clear. The route is slightly confused by the existence of other tracks but the line you should take veers to the left and takes you up and over the eastern flank of Tyle Du.

As the track rises, the limestone crags and quarries of Carreg Yr Ogof come into view.

Carreg Yr Ogof is a Carboniferous Limestone outcrop, and as the name implies there is a cave in its vicinity. You can see the ruins of a number of limekilns.

The track drops down a little and fords the head of the Nant yr Ysgwydd stream. Having crossed the stream leave the bridleway track and veer right along a narrow sheep track to begin the ascent of Carreg Yr Ogof.

There is no one clearly defined track to the summit, but the greensward is good to walk on and the limestone crags are easy to surmount. Once on the summit plateau go to its western side and locate the trig point pillar (SN777214).

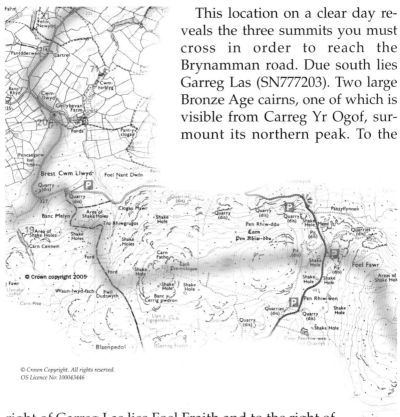

This location on a clear day reveals the three summits you must cross in order to reach the Brynamman road. Due south lies Garreg Las (SN777203). Two large Bronze Age cairns, one of which is visible from Carreg Yr Ogof, surmount its northern peak. To the

right of Garreg Las lies Foel Fraith and to the right of that is Garreg Lwyd.

North of Carreg yr Ogof, in the direction of Twynllanan, there is a cottage called Beili Glas. It was the childhood home of the writer Richard Vaughan, author of 'Moulded in Earth' and 'Son of Justin'. Both books describe life in the area in the 19th century. He wrote many other books, but it was 'Moulded in Earth' and 'Son of Justin' that made him famous in his lifetime when they were turned into a successful television series. If you can find copies, do read them. They add a layer of meaning to the understanding of this remote area.

To Carreg Las

From Carreg Yr Ogof head due south and aim for the prominent cairn on the summit of Garreg Las. There is a deep valley between you and Garreg Las, which is not obvious from the map. If you veer right you can go round the head of the valley and avoid losing much height.

There are several minor tracks leading to Garreg Las. You are certain to connect up with one to make your progress easier.

If you are attempting this section of the route in mist or fog it is essential that you locate the two cairns. If you have trouble retrace your steps and use the road route.

When you reach the summit go round to the left of the cairns and having passed the second wheel round to the right, cross two short areas of angular millstone grit rocks and connect with the track that runs just west of south along the western edge of the summit ridge.

This linear track is at times not very distinct but locating it makes all the difference between a comfortable traverse of the ridge and an ankle-bending stumble.

The ridge is characterised by a very rough terrain of millstone grit rocks and boulders. There are deep gullies resembling miniature canyons. Only the western edge offers a reasonable passage.

But beware in wet or damp conditions. These rocks can be slippery and should be crossed with caution.

East of Garreg Las, among the tumble of rocks below the summit, there are two partially completed millstone wheels (SN779203). These wheels probably date from the period of the Napoleonic Wars when the supply of millstone from Brittany ceased due to the war. Certainly, they were made not later than 1830.

You will be walking along the western edge of the ridge for about 1.25 miles, 2 km. Eventually the rocky surface becomes grassy as the track descends.

To Foel Fraith

A clear track leads from the western edge of Carreg Las and crosses in a general westerly direction towards Foel Fraith, summit SN756183. As you walk down Garreg Las, in the area marked on the map as Godre'r Garreg Las, look out for this track across to Foel Fraith because it will indicate where you should come off Garreg Las. The chief consideration in coming off Garreg Las is to avoid crossing too wide an expanse of millstone grit rocks and boulders.

The ascent from the col between Garreg Las and Foel Fraith is only 335 feet, 102 m. However it is one of those hills with many false summits and when you get to the top there is no one obvious high point. Instead it is an area of sink holes and bogs. The summit plateau is very uneven and it seems some time before you reach a point where you actually start to descend on the other side. In fact it may not be until you start to descend that your next destination, Garreg Lwyd, becomes visible.

To Carreg Lwyd

There is an obvious col to be crossed to reach Garreg Lwyd. You cannot miss it. There is also a good track leading across the col and continuing up the hill to the summit where you will find a large cairn and a triangulation pillar (SN740179) to confirm that you are at the summit. The path to the summit is beautifully graded and you barely notice the ascent. This is particularly surprising because it looked very steep from Foel Fraith. The descent off Garreg Lwyd presents some problem. The summit is a broad flat plateau and it is not possible to discern the next destination and therefore the direction of travel. There is a further problem. If the descent is not well planned you will have to negotiate hazardous rocks and boulders.

At the Trig Point set the compass on a north-west bearing. Proceed along that line, and as you begin to lose height your next destination will come into view. You are aiming for a car parking area at SN 732188. This will not be obvious at first but a small quarry on the western side of the road will indicate its location. However you should not head directly for it but contour around the hill until you have passed the areas with rocks and boulders. When you have done this begin the descent across short cropped grassland down to the road and the car park.

Pen Rhiw-wen to Castell Carreg Cennen

Distance: *6.2 miles/10 km*
Ascent: *500 feet/153 metres*

George Borrow walked over Pen Rhiw-wen from Llangadog in 1854. This is George Borrow's description of Pen Rhiw-wen taken from his book 'Wild Wales'. (For 'chalk' read 'limestone')

'After the turn, I had a huge chalk cliff towering over me on the right, and a chalk precipice on my left. Night was now coming on fast, and, rather to my uneasiness, masses of mist began to pour down the sides of the mountain. I hurried on, the road making frequent turnings. Presently the mist swept down upon me, and was so thick that I could only see a few yards before me. I was now obliged to slacken my pace, and to advance with some degree of caution. I moved on in this way for some time, when suddenly I heard a noise, as if a number of carts were coming rapidly down the hill. I stopped, and stood with my back close against the high bank. The noise drew nearer, and in a minute I saw indistinctly through the mist, horses, carts, and forms of men passing. In one or two cases the wheels appeared to be within a few inches of my feet. At length I gained the top, where the road turned and led down a steep descent towards the south-west. It was now quite night, and the mist was of the thickest kind. I could just see that there

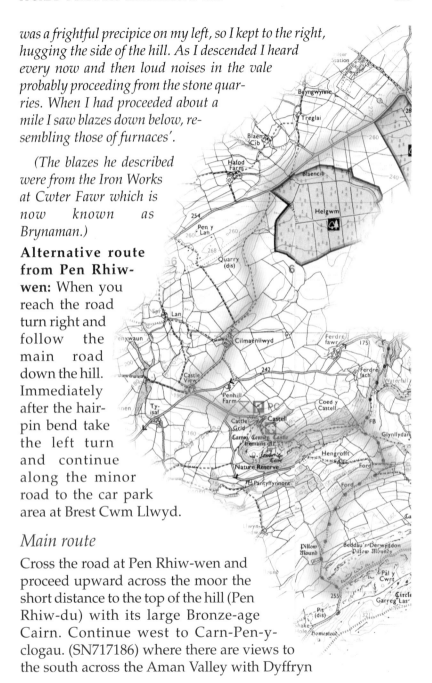

was a frightful precipice on my left, so I kept to the right, hugging the side of the hill. As I descended I heard every now and then loud noises in the vale probably proceeding from the stone quarries. When I had proceeded about a mile I saw blazes down below, resembling those of furnaces'.

(The blazes he described were from the Iron Works at Cwter Fawr which is now known as Brynaman.)

Alternative route from Pen Rhiwwen: When you reach the road turn right and follow the main road down the hill. Immediately after the hairpin bend take the left turn and continue along the minor road to the car park area at Brest Cwm Llwyd.

Main route

Cross the road at Pen Rhiw-wen and proceed upward across the moor the short distance to the top of the hill (Pen Rhiw-du) with its large Bronze-age Cairn. Continue west to Carn-Pen-y-clogau. (SN717186) where there are views to the south across the Aman Valley with Dyffryn

Tywi (The Vale of Tywi) to the north.

Immediately south of Carn Pen-y-clogau is an area called Banc-y-Cerrig-Pydron – 'bank of rottenstone'. This was one of many areas across the limestone outcrops on Mynydd Du where rottenstone was extracted, a century or two back. Rottenstone is weathered impure shale of limestone. It was ground into a powder and used for polishing and burnishing tin plate and copper manufactured in the lower Tawe Valley near Swansea. It was also exported to the English Midlands.

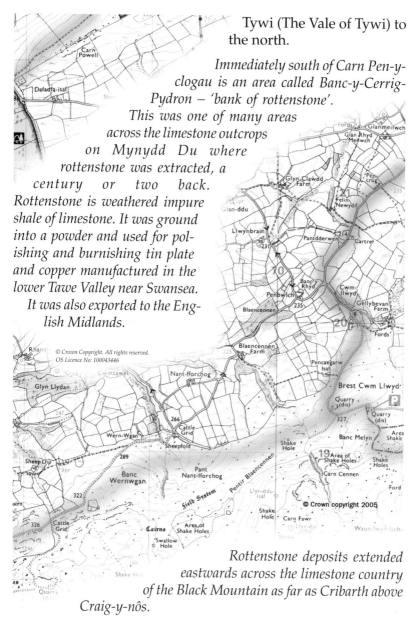

Rottenstone deposits extended eastwards across the limestone country of the Black Mountain as far as Cribarth above Craig-y-nôs.

Girls from Cwm-llynfell and Cwmtwrch would make the five mile round trip to Pen yr Helyg three times daily, weather permitting, transporting the stone by panniered ponies. The girls received one shilling

Castell Carreg Cennen is perched on the top of a 100 metre limestone crag

per journey. This stone, prior to the days of Brasso, was also used as a household metal polish.

Descend from Carn Pen-y-clogau in a westerly direction until you reach the bridleway at (SN712186). This track was once the turnpike road from Brynaman to Llangadog. Follow this old turnpike road in a northerly direction until reaching the tarmac road at Brest Cwm Llwyd.

(Alternative routes join at this point.)

On the southern side of this road are the grass covered remains of some early limekilns (SN706193). Keep on this road for a short distance until reaching the bend at SN704194. Leave the road and head for Banc Wernwgan, returning to the road at SN688191. Continue along the road in a south-westerly direction until reaching the cattle grid entering Pâl y Cwrt (SN685186).

Prior to reaching Pâl y Cwrt there is an old ruin, formerly a cultivated holding called Bryniau, close to old lime workings. The word pâl comes from the French word 'pâle' meaning enclosure. Cwrt means court: hence the 'Enclosure of the Court'. It may be that Pâl y Cwrt had been associated with Castell Carreg Cennen.

At SN675182 there are earth mounds, called Beddau'r Derwyddon. They are not the graves of the Druids as the name implies, but pillow mounds, which are mediaeval warrens for the breeding of rabbits, both for the table and their fur.

At SN 673180 turn right (heading NW) off the tarmac road at the entrance to Brondai farm. Notice a 'castle' symbol on a wooden fingerpost which directs you to Carreg Cennen along this path. After a stile by a farm gate the farm track veers to the right. Carry straight on here and go over a stile or through a metal bridleway gate straight ahead (Do not go through the metal farm gate adjacent). Follow a grassy path, fenced on both sides, (heading N) which is on the left of another farm track. The path swings right and crosses the farm track and can be very muddy as it climbs the hill. Here you will have fine views of the castle on your left. The woodland below the castle cliffs is a Site of Special Scientific Interest and is owned and managed by the National Park Authority.

At the end of this enclosed path, go over a stile by a metal gate and head down the hill in a NE direction. At a path junction, bear left, following the castle logo on the fingerpost. Towards the bottom of the hill the path veers sharp left and crosses a farm track. Here you will see a stile with 'Castle avoiding farmyard' displayed. Cross the stile (heading N) and descend to a wooden footbridge across the stream.

After another stile, you cross a more substantial wooden bridge. This was erected for the National Park Authority by Cardiff University Officer Training Corps. As you cross the bridge, you can see where willow logs have been driven into the riverbed to try and stop water eroding the bank.

Cross the bridge, turn right, and then sharp left, following the castle logo signs, up a steep grassy track, which takes you through the woodland owned by the National Park Authority, to Castell Carreg Cennen.

At the top of the hill, the Castle is well worth a visit and is open from 9.30 am to 8.00 pm (Adult admission £3). Passing the

Castell Carreg Cennen

Castle on your left, a tarmac path descends to a café/shop and then bears left to the car park and the conclusion of day 7.

There is an excellent café and shop in the old barn providing good Welsh fare. Bernard Llewellyn, the owner of the farm and castle, has a herd of old long horned cattle as well as rare breeds of sheep.

The Castle

Carreg Cennen Castle was the ancient centre and stronghold of the Commote of Is-Cennen, which lay to the south of the River Tywi, and south-east of the township of Llandeilo. This site was a stronghold long before the Norman lords recognised its strategic importance. The earliest documentary evidence for a castle on this site dates from 1248, and the existing castle belongs to the late 13th or early 14th century. It was deliberately dismantled shortly after the Wars of the Roses (in the 15th century) because it was thought too much of a threat to the monarchy.

Finds of coins on the hill dating from the 1st and 4th century suggest that the site was occupied during the Roman occupation.

The castle stands on an outlier of Carboniferous Limestone set amongst the Old Red Sandstone. The limestone crag is a zone of folding and thrusting known as the Carreg-Cennen Disturbance and is a Geological Site of Special Scientific Interest. The woodland between the castle and the river is a Local Nature Reserve.

Local Nature Reserve below Castell Carreg Cennen

DAY EIGHT

The final day:
Carreg Cennen to Garn Goch and Bethlehem
(then on to Llangadog)

Distance: *10 miles/16 km*
Ascent: *740 feet/225 metres*

HAVING made sure you visit the castle, take the road leading north-westerly to Castle View House (SN661196). From there take the north-easterly path to Cilmaenllwyd Farm (SN665199). Pass through the farm and keep on a north-easterly heading, hand railing a fence on your left. At a small stream climb some stone steps to a stile and ford the stream and then head north across a field and cross an old fence line, again, hand railing a fence on your left. After another stile an obvious path heads north-easterly by the side of a stone wall, before passing some old quarry workings. Follow the path to a ladder stile at SN 667209 and then cross a rough field (heading NNE) to arrive at a stile by a tarmac road at the corner of Helgwm forest. Turn right at the road and continue along it until reaching the cross roads at SN679218.

At the crossroads take the footpath straight ahead that goes in a north-easterly direction (north of Carn-Powell) into the forest plantation at Carreglwyd (SN687225). Continue heading north-west on a descending track through the plantation and on reaching the fence on its far side, turn sharp right and take the easterly track that rises steeply to Bwlch y Gors. Shortly after leaving the plantation, bear left along a raised embankment by the side of a new fence to cross a small stream. As you ascend, at Bwlch y Gors, there are two tracks. One goes in a north-easterly direction below Trichrug. The other, which you will take, bears left through a fence and leads down towards Bethlehem, taking a more northerly bearing. (This is, in fact, an unclassified county road.)

You might care, at Bwlch y Gors, to take a small diversion along the track and make the short ascent by the permitted path to Trichrug summit.

From this elevated position there are fine views northerly over Garn Goch and the Vale of Tywi. To the south there is the splendid view over Capel Gwynfe to the Mynydd Du. Immediately above to the east are Pen y Bicws and Trichrug at 1360 feet, 415 metres. Trichrug is a striking ridge, brought about by its tough, pebbly grits and conglomerates (laid down during the Silurian period) being resistant to erosion. The coarse pebbly conglomerates indicate the shallow-water character of the 'Trichrug Beds', probably formed by a delta pushing out into the 'Silurian Sea' from a land close by.

Due east of Trichrug at SN724233 there is farmhouse called Bailey Home Farm. This is the birthplace of Sir John Williams (1840-1926) who became the Court Physician and a principal founder of the National Library of Wales. He moved to nearby Blaen Llynant farm (SN696219) after the death of his father. He also was a pioneer in the advocacy of a Welsh National Campaign for the eradication of tuberculosis. Queen Victoria created him a baronet in 1894. He also was made K.C.V.O. in 1902 and G.C.V.O. in 1911. The Universities of Glasgow, Aberdeen and Edinburgh awarded him the honorary doctorates as did the University of Wales in 1905.

Whilst at Swansea, he began to lay the foundations of a remarkable private library of prints, and books and manuscripts in Welsh, or of Celtic interest. These he later transferred to the infant National Library of Wales at Aberystwyth.

Returning to Bwlch y Gors, follow the old grass track down to Garn-wen Farm (SN695239) which lies south-east of the Iron Age Fort of Garn-Goch. Just beyond the farm you arrive at the common. Make your way to the north-eastern entrance into this 300 BC fort. This fort is among the largest, if not the largest Iron Age Fort in Wales. It is 2296 feet, 700 metres by 656 feet, 200 metres.

Garn-Goch Iron Age Fort

There are two fine hill forts on the same hill, both of similar construction and both of the same date. A small gap divides the lower fort (Y Gaer Fach) from the main summit where the larger camp (Y Gaer Fawr) sits.

Garn Goch Iron Age Fort

The larger fort is surrounded by a massive collapsed stone rampart, which originally would have been 16 feet, 5 metres thick. There is an outer wall on the south-east side, which may be the remains of an earlier fort. In the main wall, it is possible to discern the remnants of at least six entrances, which would have been roofed over with lintels. There are the remains of a small 'postern gate' on the southern side of the main fort which is well worth a visit. The original large stones are mainly in situ. Many of them fell inwards and were re-erected in Victorian times.

The remains of the north-east entrance suggest it consisted of twin passages 50 feet, 14 metres apart. Each was 6.5 feet, 2 metres wide and 32 feet, 10 metres to 36 feet, 11 metres long, and lined with large upright slabs and roofed. The rampart was thickened for a total length of 98 feet, 30 metres. Little remains of the northern portal but a large fallen slab, at the bottom of a crater in the rubble of the rampart

There is a large stone cairn on a natural sandstone ridge in the interior of the fort. This cairn is 10 feet, 3 metres high, 180 feet, 55 metres long and 65 feet, 20 metres wide. Although it has the appearance of Neolithic Long Cairn it is almost certainly a burial cairn of Bronze Age date. During the Rebecca Riots in South-west Wales during the 19th century, Merched Becca (The Daughters of Rebecca-see below) damaged this cairn while erecting beacons upon it.

Not far from the cairn, near the middle of the fort, is a marshy area, which as recently as 1906 contained an oval pool 131 feet, 40 metres by 49 feet, 15 metres.

The western side of the rampart rises to 21 feet, 6.5 metres high while the remaining rampart is of lower height.

For a long time most of the hill has been covered with bracken. However this is soon to change. The Brecon Beacons National Park Authority owns the hill on which these two forts sit. The land, which is common land, has become the first common land to be accepted into the Tir Gofal agri-environmental scheme. This is funding a programme of bracken control, which commenced in the summer of 2004 with helicopter spraying. This should result in a dramatic reduction of the bracken. It is also planned to introduce a regime of mixed grazing, (sheep, cattle and ponies) which should prevent the re-establishment of the bracken.

For further information regarding this fine fort refer to:-
'Garn Goch, Carmarthenshire' A.H.A. Hogg.

The Daughters of Rebecca

The Daughters of Rebecca were men who dressed in women's clothing to disguise their identity. The Rebecca Riots started due to the injustices that the people had to endure from selfish landlords and excessive taxes.

The first year of Rebecca's exploits was in 1843. Their grievances were directed at the tollgates, the tithes, church rates and high rents. Sir James Graham the Home Secretary of the day in Peel's Government stated. 'I grieve to say that South Wales bids fair to rival Ireland. Poverty and misconduct of Landlords are at the root of crime and dis-

content in both countries'. Tollhouses were burnt and Tollgates destroyed. Members of Rebecca that were caught were sent to the penal colonies. But the leader of the Merched Becca was never discovered.

We continue the journey from the middle of the saddle in a westerly direction, following the ridge until the path leads down to the lane at the interpretation board for the site. At the lane turn right and after a few metres right again at the T junction downhill towards Bethlehem.

On the right of the lane is an old cattle pound recently cleared and renovated by the National Park Authority. The pound used to lock up stray animals until claimed by the owner on payment of a small fee to the parish for their keep and feed.

Follow the road until reaching Bethlehem Chapel (SN687249). Turn left at the footpath by the Chapel and cross the fields that lead to the main road and the village renowned for its Post Office, which is now a private house.

The quiet little Post Office used to be a place of great activity at Christmas. Christmas Cards posted here used to carry the Bethlehem postmark. This tradition still remains, and is carried out in the part time Post Office in the former village school (now a Community Centre). The normal opening hours are Tuesday 10 am-12 noon, Thursday 2 pm-4 pm, but as Christmas approaches all that changes. From the 1st to the 21st of December it is open Monday to Friday 10 am-4 pm and on Saturdays 10 am-12 noon.

Leave Bethlehem, continue along the road in a north-east direction and one hundred metres beyond the hill top, before the first house on the left, turn left down the bridleway through woodland to Dolau Farm. At the farm take the lane north-east through Bronallt Farm to Bryngwyn Farm and from there the field path through five fields to the hamlet of Felindre. The long journey from Abergavenny railway station is almost over. Having passed through Felindre, cross the Sawdde Bridge and the common on the southern outskirts of Llangadog to join the A4069 at Glansawdde farm.

At that road junction, if you look to the right you can see (at SN709276) the old castle Motte called Castell Meurig. This is an im-

posing Motte with a well-preserved Bailey. The impressive mound (motte) was possibly surmounted by a wooden tower, which would have formed the main defence. The main residence and the ancillary buildings of the Norman lord would have been situated in the large enclosure (bailey) to the south-west, within which a modern house has been built. This castle is also known as Castell Pridd.

Relics from the Iron Age and the Roman period have been found in the vicinity of the fort.

The Red Book of Hergest 'Brut y Tywysogion' gives a brief history of this castle for the years 1200-1208. Castell Meurig is a product the early Anglo Norman incursions into the area. The castle was captured by Prince Maelgwyn ap Rhys using catapults and slings in 1203. It was destroyed in 1209.

Walk on the road for 55 yards, 50 metres and turn left across the common for about 330 yards, 300 metres and then between gardens and houses into Llangadog, through the lanes of the village, to the main road (A4069). It's then left for the railway

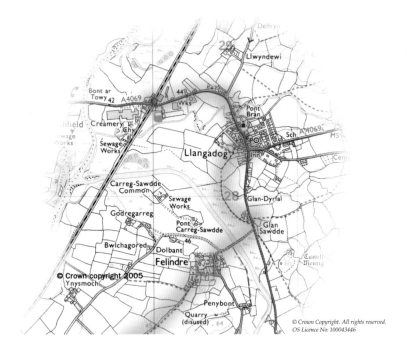

Bethlehem Post Office, the former village school

station or, right if you wish to celebrate the end of your trail to one of the five hostelries of this small village.

The small market town of Llangadog is centred on St Cadog's Church which dates from the middle ages.

The Llanelli Railway and Docks Company opened the railway through Llangadog in 1858. It was the last section of the West Wales Line — the LNWR. Miraculously this Central Wales line has managed to escape closure and trains from here travel south to Llanelli and Swansea and north to Shrewsbury.

And on reaching the station you have reached your journey's end.

Tourist Information

Information Centres — open all year

Abergavenny
Swan Meadow, Monmouth Road, Abergavenny
Monmouthshire NP7 5HH
Tel: 01873 857588
E-mail: abergavennytic@monmouthshire.gov.uk
Web: www.abergavenny.co.uk
National Park Desk: Tel: 01873 853254
Summer daily 10.00–17.30, Winter daily 10.00–16.30

Brecon
Cattle Market Square, Brecon, Powys LD3 9DA
Tel: 01874622485, E-mail: bretic@powys.gov.uk
Summer daily 09.30–17.30, Winter daily 09.30–17.00

Buith Wells
The Groe Car Park, Builth Wells, Powys LD2 3BT
Tel: 01982 553307, E-mail: builtic@powys.gov.uk
Summer and Winter daily 09.30–17.00

Craig-y-nôs Country Park
Pen-y-cae, Swansea Valley SA9 1GL
Tel: 01639 730395, E-mail: cyncp@breconbeacons.org
Web: www.breconbeacons.org
Nov-Feb 10.00-16.00 March, April & Sept Oct 10.00-1700,
May-August 10.00-18.00

Hay
The Craft Centre, Oxford Road, (by main car park)
Hay on Wye HR3 SD6
Tel: 01497 820144, E-mail: post@hay-on-wye.co.uk
Daily Summer 10.00-17.00, Winter 11.00-13.00 & 14.00-16.00

Libanus: The Mountain Centre
Tel: 01874 623366, E-mail mountain.npvc@brecombeacons.org
Open daily at 09.30, Close Mar-June 17.00, July-Aug 18.00,
Sept-Oct 17.00, Nov-Feb 16.30

Llandeilo
Car Park, Crescent Road, Llandeilo, Carmarthenshire SA19 4EU.
Tel: 01558 824226, E-mail: llandeilotic@carmarthenshire.gov.uk
Web: www.carmarthenshire.gov.uk
Summer Monday-Saturday 09.00–16.00,
Winter Saturday-Sunday 09.00–17.00

Llandovery
Heritage Centre, Kings Road, Llandovery, Carmarthenshire SA20 0AW.
Tel: 01550 720693, E-mail: llandoverytic@breconbeacons.org
Web: www.breconbeacons.org

Merthyr Tydfil
14a Glebeland Street, Merthyr Tydfil CF47 8AU
Tel: 01685 379884, E-mail: tic@merthyr.gov.uk
Monday-Saturday 09.00-16.00, Sunday closed

Information Centres — seasonal opening

Blaenavon
Blaenavon Ironworks, North Street, Blaenavon Torfaen NP4 9RQ.
Tel: 01495 792615, E-mail: blaenavon.ironworks@btopenworld.com
Summer daily 10.00-17.00

Crickhowell
Beaufort Chambers, Beaufort Street, Crickhowell, Powys NP8 1AA
Tel: 01873 812105 E-mail: cricktic@powys.gov.uk
Summer daily 09.30-17.00, Sunday 09.30-16.00

Talgarth
The Tower Shop, Talgarth LD3 0BW (in process of re-location)
Tel: 01874 712226
Easter-October

Pontneddfechan
Pontneddfechan (Pont Neath Vaughan), Nr Glynneath SA11 5NR
Tel: 01639 721795
E-mail: waterfallspontneddfechan@hotmail.com
Easter–October 09.30-17.30, Winter Saturday & Sunday 10.00-17.00

Brecon Beacons National Park Authority Visitor Services

Visit the web site:

www.breconbeacons.org for information about all aspects of the National Park.

Enquiries may be made directly to:

Visitor Services Department, Brecon Beacons National Park Authority, Plas y Ffynnon, Cambrian Way, Brecon, Powys LD3 7HP

Tel: 01874 624437, E-mail: enquiries@breconbeacons.org

Web: www.breconbeacons.org

Office hours: 08.30 -17.00 Monday-Friday

The Brecon Beacons National Park Authority has Information Centres at the following locations:

Open all year

Abergavenny, The National Park Visitor Centre, Libanus, Craig-y-nôs Country Park, Llandovery.

Public transport

The Tourist Information Centres will provide up to date information on public transport. However, visitors need to be aware, that as with most rural areas, there is not much of it about. So check it out very carefully.

Sunday travel presents some problems

In recent years the Brecon Beacons National Park Authority has received grant aid to provide an extensive Sunday service during the summer months. The routes taken in and around the Park provide transport links unavailable during the week. The routes and the timetable vary from year to year. It is a very good and useful service and information is available from Tourist Information Centres and from the head office of the National Park Authority and on the Website www.visitbreconbeacons.com

Sumary of main services available

Note: These are subject to change.

Locations on the direct route of the Beacons Way, or near to it, are shown in red.

Abergavenny
Train Services
North to Hereford, Shrewsbury, Manchester with links to Birmingham etc.

South to Newport and Cardiff for connections to London, the West Country etc.

Bus Services
West to Brecon along A40 calling at Crickhowell, Bwlch, Talybont.

North to Hereford.

South and south-west to Newport & Cardiff. Buses go via Heads of Valleys road as well as Cwmbran.

East to Monmouth.

Brecon
Bus Services
To Abergavenny (see Abergavenny above).

To Hereford via Talgarth and Hay on Wye.

To Llandovery via Senny Bridge. At Llandovery connections may be made for Llangadog and the mid Wales railway line.

To Craig-y-nôs via Senny Bridge and south to Swansea.

To Merthyr Tydfil via Libanus and Storey Arms (and then by bus or train to Cardiff etc).

Limited service to Builth.

Craig-y-nôs
Bus Services
To Swansea and Brecon

Llandovery
Train Services
On Heart of Wales Line
Trains to Swansea via
Llangadog and through to Shrewsbury

Bus Services
To Brecon via Senny Bridge
To Llandeilo where there are connections to Swansea and West Wales
Limited service to Lampeter

Llangadog
Train Services
Heart of Wales Line Trains to Llandovery through to Shrewsbury and south to Swansea.

Bus Services
South to Llandeilo where there are bus connections and north to Llandovery where there is a connection to Brecon.

Taxis
The local information offices centres will be able to advise you, as will the National Park Travel Guide. This guide is also available at www.visitbreconbeacons.com

Mobile Phones: A warning
Visitors are reminded that because of the mountainous terrain mobile phones do not operate in large areas of the Brecon Beacons National Park. This is particularly important if walkers are planning to contact car drivers or taxis to pick them up at the end of the day. There are public telephone boxes at or near the end of all sections of the Trail.

Accommodation
The Tourist Information Offices, particularly those open throughout the year, are the most useful source of information concerning the range of accommodation available.

The Brecon Beacons Park Society's Website:
www.breconbeaconsparksociety.org will also carry information concerning accommodation en-route.

The Youth Hostels on route, at Llwyn y Celyn – below Pen y Fan (tel 01874 624261) and Llanddeusant (tel 01550 740218) are very popular and you are advised to book well in advance.

Some further reading

These publications listed below (and others named in the text) were consulted during the writing of this guide.

'Brecon Beacons National Park National Park Guide No. 5'
Her Majesty's Stationery Office 1978.

Out of print but worth searching for. The most comprehensive guide to the Brecon Beacons National Park.

'Brecon Beacons. The Official National Park Guide'
Roger Thomas with photographs by Harry Williams.
Pevensey Guides 2002.

The Canals of the Welsh Valleys and their Tramroads
D.D & J.M. Gladwin
The Oakwood Press. 1991

The Brecknock and Abergavenny Canal and the many tramroads associated with it, (although not strictly in 'the valleys') are described, and their histories recorded.

Canal – The Brecon & Aergavenny (section of the Monmouthshire & Brecon) Canal
John Norris
John Norris, The Birches, off Wickham Hill, Hurstpierpoint, West Sussex. BN6 9NP

A very comprehensive guide to the canal written primarily for boat users but of equal interest to walkers.

Carreg Cennen Castle
CADW 1990
The Official Guide

Classic Landforms of the Brecon Beacons
Richard Shakesby
The British Geomorphological Research Group. 2002
A 45 page superbly illustrated account of the formation of the landforms in the Black Mountain (Mynydd Du), Fforest Fawr and Central Brecon Beacons.

Hills and Vales of the Black Mountain District
Richard Baker-Gabb
First published 1913. Reprinted by Lapridge Publications.
Tel: 01432 353586

Still available from bookshops. A very informative, interesting and useful account of the Monmouthshire Black Mountains.

Llanthony Priory
O.E. Craster. TD, MA, FSA
Her Majesty's Stationery Office 1963
Department of the Environment Official Handbook

Mynydd Du and Fforest Fawr – The Evolution of an Uplands Landscape in South Wales.
David K. Leighton
Royal Commission on the Ancient and Historical Monuments of Wales. 1997
This account explores the history of human activity in the western upland area of the National Park from the end of the last glaciation to the present.

Powys – The Buildings of Wales
Richard Haslam
Penguin and University of Wales Press. 1979

Prehistoric Peoples – their life and legacy
Peter Dorling and David Brinn
Brecon Beacons National Park. 1996

Shadows in a Landscape. Llangynidr. The Evolution of a Community.
Published by Llangynidr Local History Society 2000
An account of the history, life and landscape of a Breconshire village and the countryside around it.

Stone and Steam in the Black Mountains
David Tipper
Blorenge Books 1975, reprint 1994
The classic account of the building of the Grwynefawr Reservoir in the Monmouthshire Black Mountains.

Guidebooks

In recent years the interest in walking has much increased. Walking magazines are flourishing. National and local trails have been created, and there has never been such a selection of walking guides available. Given this abundance, it is difficult to make a choice. Listed below are some of the titles currently available.

Aircraft crash sites and the stories behind them
Brecon Beacons National Park Authority

Brecon Beacons and Glamorgan Walks
Pathfinder Guide
Jarrold

Circular Walks in the Brecon Beacons National Park
Tom Hutton
Gwasg Carreg Gwalch 1998

Classic Walks in the Brecon Beacons National Park
Chris Barber
Blorenge Books 2000

Walks in the Craig-y-nôs area and Upper Tawe Valley
Brecon Beacons National Park Authority

Walks from Abergavenny
Brecon Beacons National Park Authority

Walks from The Mountain Centre
Brecon Beacons National Park Authority

Waterside Places
Brecon Beacons National Park Authority

Many of the walking guidebooks to the Brecon Beacons National Park can be purchased from Tourist Information Centres in the Brecon Beacons National Park.

Cymdeithas Parc Bannau Brycheiniog
The Brecon Beacons Park Society

The Brecon Beacons National Park is an area of outstandingly beautiful countryside dominated by mountains and moorland rising above peaceful valleys dotted with farms and woods. It contains within a relatively small space remarkably diverse landforms and habitats.

The Park Society is an independent organisation for anyone who cares about and enjoys this very special landscape and environment.

Our ever-growing membership consists of people living both within and outside the Park who wish to see its essential characteristics conserved or enhanced. They are people who wish to know more about its past present and future.

Every week the Park Society stages at least two events which explore on foot these protected landscapes. The Park Society is simply the best way to learn more about The Brecon Beacons National Park.

For more information visit our website which contains any updates on The Beacons Way and application forms for the Society:

www.breconbeaconsparksociety.org

Walking Wales Magazine is published quarterly
by Walking Wales Magazine Ltd

If you would like to become a subscriber write to
Walking Walking Magazine, FREEPOST NWW16824
Machynlleth SY20 8ZB

Tel & Fax: 01650 511314